Veggie chic

hamlyn

Veggie chic

Rose Elliot

First published in Great Britain in 2006 by
Hamlyn, a division of Octopus Publishing Group Ltd
2–4 Heron Quays, London E14 4JP

Copyright © Octopus Publishing Group Ltd 2006
Text copyright © Rose Elliot 2006

Distributed in the United States and Canada by
Sterling Publishing Co., Inc.
387 Park Avenue South, New York, NY 10016-8810

ISBN-13: 978-0-600-61566-8
ISBN-10: 0-600-61566-9

A CIP catalogue record for this book is available
from the British Library

Printed and bound in China

10 9 8 7 6 5 4 3 2 1

Buy cheese with the vegetarian symbol to ensure it is made with vegetarian rennet and buy vegetarian Parmesan-style cheese instead of traditional Parmesan which is not vegetarian. Always check the labels of preprepared ingredients to make sure they do not contain non-vegetarian ingredients such as gelatin.

Notes

Ovens should be preheated to the specified temperature. If using a fan-assisted oven, follow the manufacturer's instructions for adjusting the temperature. This usually means reducing the temperature by 65°F. Broilers should also be preheated.

Free-range medium eggs should be used unless otherwise specified. The Department of Health and Human Services advises that eggs should not be consumed raw. This book contains some dishes made with raw or lightly cooked eggs. It is prudent for more vulnerable people, such as pregnant and nursing mothers, invalids, the elderly, babies and young children, to avoid uncooked or lightly cooked dishes made with eggs.

Vegan recipes are labelled

Fresh herbs should be used unless otherwise stated. If unavailable use dried herbs as an alternative but halve the quantities stated.

This book includes dishes made with nuts and nut derivatives. It is advisable for those with known allergic reactions to nuts and nut derivatives and those who may be potentially vulnerable to these allergies, such as pregnant and nursing mothers, invalids, the elderly, babies and children, to avoid dishes made with nuts and nut oils. It is also prudent to check the labels of preprepared ingredients for the possible inclusion of nut derivatives.

Salt and pepper: use sea salt and freshly ground black pepper, unless otherwise specified.

contents

introduction

When I was asked to write this book I was thrilled. I've been wanting to write a "decadent" vegetarian cookbook for some time, to show just how luxurious and delectable the food can be, and to address the perennial question "what can I do for vegetarian entertaining?," and here was my chance. But veggie *chic*? What exactly did that mean?

The dictionary was consulted: "elegant and stylishly fashionable; graceful," it said; "pleasingly ingenious and simple." A picture was emerging: recipes that were a bit different—fresh, bold, stunning yet simple. They also had to be easily achievable, because to me "chic" also implies confidence, ease, and effortlessness. And definitely have a bit of the "wow factor." When I've spent time and energy cooking a special meal, one of the joys, apart from the taste of the food and the pleasure of the company, are the "oohs" and "ahs" that greet the dishes—and the empty plates at the end of the meal. What cook doesn't love that?

I set about inventing, testing, and tasting what I hoped were "pleasantly ingenious and simple" dishes. I had a lot of fun creating these and many memorable meals. Some were simple. There was the evening

when I made the Mixed Mushroom Tempura and we all sat around the kitchen table, glasses of wine in hand, trying the crispy golden morsels, hot and crunchy, straight out of the pan, with various dips to see which went best. Well, that was the excuse...

Different, but equally successful, was the party when I wanted to try out as many of the recipes as I could. The Baby Yorkshire Puddings with Nut Roast and Horseradish were the undisputed stars of that party and deserve special mention. They definitely passed the "wow factor" test, but in fact everything in that section of the book—Party time—passed the "not a crumb left" test.

Another unforgettable occasion was the summer feast when we had the Bloody Mary Jello followed by Salad of Warm Artichokes and Chanterelles, then the Individual Pea, Spinach, and Mint Pithiviers, with a final flourish provided by the Pink Champagne Granita Marbled with Raspberries. That menu may sound a bit daunting, yet when you analyze it, each of the four courses is actually quite simple and a lot of the preparation can be done in advance—one of the keys to successful and stress-free entertaining.

When I was working on this book I tested the

recipes on whoever happened to be around. People tried them, gave me their opinion and recipes were changed and adapted accordingly. So the recipes don't belong to some special "chic" group: they have general appeal and can be made by anyone with average kitchen skills.

They can also be adapted to suit the occasion. For instance, you'll find that the majority of the recipes have a simplicity about them and also allow for advance preparation. The Rice Noodles with Chili-Ginger Vegetables, for instance, the Squash Stuffed with Moroccan Rice, the Bubble-and-Squeak Cakes with Beet Relish, the Portobello Steaks en Croûte—these, and others like them, are easy to do. You can serve them just with a salad or a vegetable accompaniment, or you can build them into a fantastic menu of several courses, if you wish.

Alternatively, go for drama with a stunning centerpiece such as the Chickpea Flatcake Topped with Lemon- and Honey-Roasted Vegetables, the Potato and White Truffle Torte, or the Dauphinoise Roulade with Red Chard and Dolcelatte Filling. There are so many possibilities; how simple or showy, relaxed or formal you make the feast is up to you.

My advice is this: whatever you are cooking and for whatever occasion, whether it's rustling up a quick meal for one or two after work, or preparing a five-course dinner for ten, cook what you love to eat. If you're entertaining, get organized as much as you can in advance—and if you're nervous, or want to spend the maximum time with your guests, choose dishes that can mostly be made ahead. Then—and this is most important—relax and have fun!

Remember, there's so much more to food than just ingredients and recipes. It's also about pleasure, generosity, warmth, and sharing, not whether you've got everything absolutely restaurant-perfect (you eat out for that). It's the spirit behind it that counts, that's what makes food healing, soothing, bonding, cheering, uplifting, and nourishing for the soul as well as for the body, and what will make your food special. Giving others pleasure through the food you cook must be one of the simplest yet most profound joys there is.

Rose Elliot

amazing appetizers and side dishes

The perfect appetizer awakens and tantalizes

the taste buds ready for the delights of

the main course—and is easy to make,

with most of the preparation done in advance.

These recipes fit the bill and there are also

some delectable side dishes which really

complement the main course.

hot pomegranate and pecan leafy salad

nuts leaves seeds oil

(V)

serves 4
preparation 10 minutes
cooking 12 minutes

1 cup pecan nuts, roughly broken
1 tablespoon balsamic vinegar
2 tablespoons olive oil
5 cups peppery leaves, such as
    arugula or watercress
1 pomegranate
salt and pepper, to taste

1 Spread the pecan nuts out on a baking sheet and place in a preheated oven, 350°F, for about 12 minutes, or until lightly browned and aromatic. Remove from the oven and tip onto a plate to prevent them from burning.

2 Mix the balsamic vinegar, olive oil, and some salt and pepper in a large salad bowl to make a dressing.

3 Put the leaves on top of the dressing, but don't toss them. Halve the pomegranate as you would a grapefruit and turn the skin inside out to make the seeds pop out. Add the seeds to the leaves, along with the pecans.

4 Toss the salad and serve immediately.

wakame, cucumber, and scallion salad with rice vinegar

sesame wakame mirin

(V)

serves 4
preparation 10 minutes,
  plus soaking

¼ oz wakame seaweed
½ cucumber, peeled and shredded
6 scallions, chopped
1 tablespoon rice vinegar
1 tablespoon mirin (or a dash of
  honey for non-vegans)
1 tablespoon shoyu or tamari
salt, pepper, and sugar, to taste
a few toasted sesame seeds

1 Put the wakame into a bowl, cover with boiling water and allow to soak for 10 minutes, then drain and chop or snip.

2 Put the cucumber and scallions into a bowl. Add the wakame, rice vinegar, mirin or honey, and the shoyu or tamari, mix gently and season with salt, pepper, and sugar.

3 Put the salad into a shallow dish or onto individual plates and scatter with a few toasted sesame seeds. Serve at once.

stilton and cherry salad with cinnamon dressing

cherries stilton sherry

serves 4
**preparation 10 minutes,
   plus marinating**

⅓ cup dried cherries
2 tablespoons sherry, port, or other
   fortified wine
1 large lettuce, torn, or about
   12 cups mixed salad leaves
2 oz blue Stilton, crumbled
½ cup slivered almonds, toasted

for the cinnamon dressing
4 tablespoons olive oil
2 tablespoons raspberry vinegar
2 teaspoons superfine sugar
1 teaspoon ground cinnamon
Tabasco, salt, and pepper, to taste

1 Put the dried cherries into a small container, cover with the sherry or port and set aside to plump up—if you can leave them for a few hours, so much the better.

2 To make the dressing, beat together the olive oil, raspberry vinegar, sugar, cinnamon, and several drops of Tabasco—enough to give it a good kick—and some salt and pepper.

3 Put the lettuce or salad leaves into a bowl with the Stilton, almonds, and cherries, together with any of their liquid that remains. Drizzle over the cinnamon dressing and toss gently. Serve at once.

I adapted this salad from one served by Chef Robert Bruce in New Orleans. It has a very warming, festive feel.

salad of warm artichokes and chanterelles

butter garlic chives

serves 4
preparation 30 minutes
cooking 50 minutes

4 globe artichokes, stems removed
2 tablespoons olive oil
2 tablespoons butter
8 oz chanterelle mushrooms
4 garlic cloves, finely chopped
squeeze of lemon juice
1 red oak-leaf lettuce
chopped chives
salt and pepper, to taste

for the vinaigrette dressing
2 tablespoons balsamic vinegar
6 tablespoons extra virgin olive oil

1 Cover the artichokes in boiling water and cook for about 45 minutes, or until a leaf will pull off easily. Drain and rinse under cold water to cool quickly. Pull off the leaves until you get to the central fluffy "choke," then pull this off gently with your fingers under a cold running tap and discard. Slice the bases thickly and set aside.

2 To prepare the dressing, put the balsamic vinegar, olive oil, and a generous seasoning of salt in a lidded jar and shake until combined.

3 Just before you want to serve the salad, heat the olive oil and butter in a skillet and add the chanterelles and garlic. Cook for a few minutes until they are tender and any liquid has been reabsorbed. Add the sliced artichoke bases and cook for 1–2 minutes to heat them through, stirring often. Season well with a squeeze of lemon juice and some salt and pepper.

4 While the mushrooms are cooking, arrange some oak-leaf lettuce leaves on 4 plates and drizzle with the dressing. Spoon the chanterelle and artichoke mixture on top and scatter with chopped chives. Serve at once.

Provided you have a couple of large saucepans, I think it's easier to cook the artichokes whole and then remove the leaves and choke, rather than trimming them first.

salsify fritters with caper cream

lemon sour cream

serves 4
preparation 30 minutes
cooking 20 minutes

1 lb 8 oz salsify or scorzonera
2 tablespoons freshly squeezed
   lemon juice
1 tablespoon olive oil
1 tablespoon red wine vinegar
2 large eggs, beaten
flour for coating
¾ dried bread crumbs
canola or peanut oil for deep-frying
salt and pepper, to taste
lemon wedges, to serve

for the caper cream
2 tablespoons mayonnaise
2 tablespoons sour cream or
   crème fraîche
1 tablespoon capers, rinsed

1 Wearing gloves to protect your hands (the juice can stain), peel the salsify or scorzonera under a cold running tap, cut it into about 1¼ inch lengths and put in a saucepan of water containing 1 tablespoon of the lemon juice. Don't worry if you can't remove all the skin—some tiny flecks don't matter.

2 Boil the pieces in the water for about 10 minutes, or until tender, then drain and add the remaining lemon juice, the olive oil, red wine vinegar, and some salt and pepper. Allow to cool.

3 Meanwhile, make the caper cream. Mix the mayonnaise with the sour cream or crème fraîche and capers and season with salt and pepper.

4 Dip each piece of salsify or scorzonera into the beaten egg, then into flour, then into the egg again and finally into the bread crumbs, to coat all over.

5 Heat the oil to 350–375°F, or until a cube of bread browns in 30 seconds, and deep-fry the coated pieces for about 3 minutes, or until they are crisp and golden brown. Drain on paper towels and serve at once, garnished with lemon wedges and accompanied by the caper cream.

Salsify is a long, slim root with a dark skin and creamy white flesh within, and scorzorena is similar. If you can't find either of these, you could use canned salsify. Either way, the texture and flavor are delicate and delicious.

hot and sour mushroom soup

lime cilantro ginger

(V)

serves 4
preparation 10 minutes,
plus standing
cooking 15–20 minutes

1 teaspoon vegetarian Thai red
  curry paste
4 oz shiitake mushrooms,
  thinly sliced
1 small cluster enoki mushrooms,
  base trimmed off
1 red chili, seeded and cut
  into rings
⅓ cup chopped cilantro
juice of 1 lime
2–3 tablespoons shoyu or tamari
salt, to taste

for the Thai-flavored stock
2–3 lemon grass stalks, crushed
  with a rolling pin
6 kaffir lime leaves, plus 6 more
  to garnish (optional)
stems from a small bunch of
  fresh cilantro
2 thumb-size pieces of fresh
  ginger root, peeled and sliced
4 cups water

1 To make the stock, put the lemon grass, lime leaves, cilantro stems, and ginger into a saucepan with the water. Bring to a boil, then reduce the heat and simmer for 10 minutes. Remove from the heat, cover the pan and allow to stand for 30 minutes or longer for the flavors to infuse, then drain the liquid into another pan and discard the flavorings.

2 Add the curry paste, mushrooms, and red chili to the stock, then reheat and simmer for 3–4 minutes, to cook the mushrooms and chili.

3 Stir in the chopped cilantro, lime juice, shoyu or tamari, and some salt, then reheat gently. Serve in individual bowls and garnish with a lime leaf, if desired.

This glamorous soup has a long list of ingredients but is incredibly quick to make! Use a medium-size, long chili for this—not the tiny, very hot bird's eye type. Make sure the curry paste is vegetarian—read the label.

creamy fennel soup with gremolata

fennel parsley cream

serves 4
preparation 15 minutes
cooking 20 minutes

2 large fennel bulbs, trimmed
  and sliced
1 onion, roughly chopped
3¾ cups vegetable stock
6 tablespoons heavy cream
salt and pepper, to taste

for the gremolata
2 tablespoons chopped parsley
thinly pared or finely grated zest
  of ½ lemon
1 garlic clove, finely chopped

1 Gently simmer the fennel and onion in the stock for 15–20 minutes, until very tender.

2 To make the gremolata, mix all the ingredients in a bowl and set aside.

3 Blend the fennel, onion, and stock in a food processor or using an immersion blender, and for an ultra-smooth result pass the soup through a strainer.

4 Add the cream to the soup and season with salt and pepper, then ladle the soup into warmed bowls and top each with a spoonful of gremolata to serve.

butternut squash and orange soup with nutmeg

serves 4
preparation 15 minutes
cooking 35 minutes

1 butternut squash, halved and
   seeded
2 onions, chopped
2 tablespoons olive oil
2 garlic cloves, chopped
juice and grated zest of 1 orange
¼ teaspoon ground nutmeg
3¾ cups water
salt and pepper, to taste
chopped parsley, to garnish

1 Put the squash, cut-side down, on a lightly greased baking sheet and bake in a preheated oven, 400°F, for 30 minutes, or until tender.

2 Meanwhile, cook the onions in the olive oil in a covered pan over a gentle heat for about 10 minutes, until tender. Stir in the garlic and cook for an additional 1–2 minutes.

3 Scoop out the flesh from the butternut squash halves and mix with the onions and garlic, orange juice and zest, nutmeg, and some salt and pepper. Puree using an immersion blender or food processor, adding a little of the water if necessary.

4 Tip the mixture into a saucepan with enough of the water to make a creamy consistency and heat gently.

5 Serve garnished with chopped parsley.

chilled melon soup with mint granita

lemon mint melon

V

serves 4
preparation 20 minutes,
**   plus chilling and freezing**
cooking 5 minutes

1 ripe ogen melon
superfine sugar, to taste

for the mint granita
½ cup superfine sugar
large bunch of mint
1¼ cups water
1 tablespoon freshly squeezed
   lemon juice

1 Remove the skin and seeds from the melon and cut the flesh into chunks. Puree in a food processor until very smooth. Taste and add a little sugar if necessary, then chill.

2 To make the granita, put the sugar, mint, and water into a saucepan and heat gently until the sugar has dissolved, then bring to a boil. Remove from the heat, cover, and leave until cold.

3 Once cold, remove the mint and squeeze it to extract all the liquid. Save about a dozen leaves and discard the rest. Puree the liquid with the reserved leaves and add the lemon juice. Pour into a suitable container and freeze until firm. Remove from the freezer 20–30 minutes before serving, to allow the granita to soften a little.

4 To serve, ladle the melon soup into chilled bowls. Beat the frozen mint mixture with a fork (or whiz chunks briefly in a food processor) and add a scoop to each bowl. Serve at once.

rosemary sorbet

wine rosemary lemon

(V)

serves 4
preparation 15 minutes,
   plus cooling and freezing
cooking 2 minutes

⅔ cup water
⅔ cup superfine sugar
5 sprigs of rosemary
1 cup white wine
4 tablespoons freshly squeezed
   lemon juice
a few small sprigs and flowers
   of rosemary, to decorate (optional)

1 Put the water and sugar into a saucepan with 4 sprigs of rosemary and bring to a boil. Remove from the heat, cover, and set aside to cool and infuse the flavor of the rosemary.

2 Remove the rosemary from the cooled syrup and stir in the wine and lemon juice. Chop the remaining sprig of rosemary and stir in.

3 Pour the mixture into a shallow container and freeze for about 2 hours, or until firm, scraping down the sides and beating as it solidifies. Alternatively, freeze in an ice-cream maker until the mixture is soft and slushy, then transfer to a plastic container and freeze until required.

4 Remove the sorbet from the freezer about 15 minutes before you want to serve it, then scoop it into bowls and decorate with rosemary sprigs and flowers, if desired.

Serve as a light appetizer or as a palate refresher between courses. Be warned—it's quite alcoholic.

eggplant and mozzarella scallops

cheese tomatoes onion

serves 4
preparation 20 minutes
cooking 30 minutes

1 fat eggplant, stem trimmed
olive oil, for brushing
3 oz mozzarella cheese
1 egg, beaten
dried bread crumbs for coating
canola or peanut oil for deep-frying
salt and pepper, to taste

for the tomato sauce
1 onion, chopped
1 tablespoon olive oil
2 garlic cloves, finely chopped
13 oz can chopped tomatoes

1 First make the tomato sauce. Fry the onion in the olive oil with a lid on the pan for about 8 minutes, until almost tender. Add the garlic and cook for an additional 2 minutes, then stir in the tomatoes and cook, uncovered, for about 20 minutes, or until very thick. Puree in a food processor or blender, then season and set aside.

2 For the scallops, cut 20 rounds from the eggplant, making them as thin as you can—about ⅛ inch if possible. Brush them on both sides with olive oil and cook under a hot broiler for about 5 minutes, or until tender but not browned. Season them with salt and pepper.

3 Cut the mozzarella into 20 cubes, put one cube in the center of an eggplant disk and fold the eggplant over like a mini turnover to make a "scallop." Dip in beaten egg and dried bread crumbs. Repeat with the remaining eggplant. Put the coated eggplant scallops on a piece of nonstick paper and chill until required.

4 Heat the oil to 350–375°F, or until a cube of bread browns in 30 seconds, and deep-fry the eggplant scallops until crisp and golden all over, turning them as necessary. Drain on paper towels.

5 Serve 5 on each plate, with the tomato sauce drizzled around the edge.

Morsels of mozzarella wrapped in thin eggplant slices, crumbed and deep-fried, make a tasty appetizer, served with tomato sauce.

spinach custards with avocado

nutmeg spinach eggs

serves 4
preparation 20 minutes
cooking 35–40 minutes

butter, for greasing
6 cups spinach
1¼ cups heavy cream
2 eggs
1 large ripe avocado
grated nutmeg, salt, and pepper,
   to taste

for the lemon vinaigrette
3 tablespoons freshly squeezed
   lemon juice
9 tablespoons olive oil

1 Grease 4 x ½ cup ramekins, cups, individual pudding basins, or other suitable molds with butter and line the base of each with a circle of nonstick paper.

2 Wash the spinach, then place in a saucepan with just the water clinging to it and cook for about 6 minutes, or until very tender. Drain well in a strainer, squeezing out as much water as possible, then chop.

3 Put the spinach into a food processor with the cream and eggs and whiz to a puree, then season with grated nutmeg, salt, and pepper.

4 Pour the mixture into the greased molds, stand these in a roasting pan, and pour boiling water around them. Bake in a preheated oven, 350°F, for 30 minutes, or until firm on top and a toothpick inserted into the center comes out clean. Remove from the oven and allow to cool.

5 To make the vinaigrette, whisk the lemon juice with the olive oil and some salt and pepper.

6 Slip a knife around the edges of the molds to loosen, then turn them out onto individual plates. Peel and slice the avocado and arrange some slices on each plate. Season with salt and pepper, then spoon the lemon vinaigrette over the avocado and the custards and serve warm or cold.

hot hazelnut-coated vignotte with red currant relish

serves 4
preparation 10 minutes
cooking 5 minutes

2 x 6 oz Vignotte or Brie-type
   cheese
⅔ cup skinned hazelnuts, chopped
1 egg, beaten
salad leaves and vinaigrette
   dressing (see page 15)

for the red currant relish
⅔ cup redcurrants
1 tablespoon superfine sugar
squeeze of lemon juice

1 Remove any labels stuck on the cheeses, then cut them widthwise into 4 rounds, retaining the rind. Spread the hazelnuts out on a plate.

2 Dip the rounds of cheese first in the beaten egg then into the hazelnuts, making sure that all surfaces are thickly coated. Put the pieces of coated cheese on a sheet of nonstick paper and chill until required.

3 To make the relish, heat the red currants with the sugar and lemon juice. Bring to a boil, then remove from the heat and set aside.

4 Just before you want to serve the meal, transfer the cheese to a baking sheet and cook, rind side down, under a hot broiler for about 5 minutes, or until the nuts are crisp and golden brown. Gently reheat the red currant relish.

5 While the cheese is cooking, line 4 plates with a few salad leaves and drizzle them with a little of the vinaigrette.

6 Serve the sizzling pieces of cheese on top of the leaves, with some of the red currant relish spooned on top and the rest in a small bowl.

bloody mary jellos

vodka tomato celery

serves 4
preparation 15 minutes,
   plus setting
cooking 2 minutes

1¾ cups tomato juice
1 teaspoon vegetarian gelatin
1½ tablespoons freshly squeezed
   lemon juice
6 tablespoons vodka
2 teaspoons vegetarian
   Worcestershire sauce
   (see page 185)
½ teaspoon Tabasco
2 tablespoons each finely chopped
   red onion, celery, and green
   sweet pepper, plus a little more
   chopped red onion and celery,
   to garnish
1 tablespoon horseradish sauce
3 tablespoons light cream
salt and pepper, to taste

1 Put the tomato juice into a saucepan, gradually scatter the gelatin over the cold juice and stir until it has dissolved. Slowly bring to a boil, then remove from the heat immediately and stir in the lemon juice, vodka, Worcestershire sauce, Tabasco, and some salt and pepper.

2 Divide the chopped vegetables between 4 small bowls or glasses. Pour the tomato jello on top and allow to set for at least 30 minutes. Cool until required but don't refrigerate.

3 To serve, mix the horseradish sauce with the cream and swirl some over the top of each jello. Scatter a little chopped red onion and celery over each one to garnish.

These are best made not too far in advance and kept in a cool place rather than in the refrigerator. This recipe can be vegan if you use non-dairy horseradish sauce and soy cream from a healthfood store.

tomato and parmesan tarts with basil cream

serves 4
**preparation 15 minutes,
plus standing for the basil
cream, if possible**
cooking 35 minutes

12 oz frozen ready-rolled all-butter
puff pastry (see page 184)
¼ cup grated Parmesan-style
cheese
2 cups cherry tomatoes, halved
2 teaspoons superfine sugar
salt and pepper, to taste

for the basil cream
bunch of basil, stems removed,
leaves lightly chopped
6 tablespoons light cream or
olive oil

1 To make the basil cream, mix the basil with the cream or olive oil, season with a little salt and pepper and set aside—this gets better and better as it stands, so can be made some hours in advance if convenient.

2 Spread the pastry out on a board and cut into circles to fit 4 inch diameter shallow tart pans with removable bases.

3 Put the pastry into the tart pans and trim the edges as necessary. Prick the pastry all over with a fork. Bake in a preheated oven, 400°F, for 15 minutes until golden brown—the pastry will puff up, so press it down gently with the back of a spoon. Remove the tart cases from the oven.

4 Sprinkle the Parmesan over the top of the tarts—this keeps the pastry dry and crisp. Toss the tomatoes with the sugar and some salt and pepper and divide them between the tart cases—fill them generously as the tomatoes will shrink a bit as they cook.

5 Put the tarts back into the oven and bake for 20 minutes. Remove the tarts from their pans, place on warmed plates, and swirl some of the basil cream over the top of each one. Serve at once.

crisp tofu with tomato and lemon grass sambal

chili garlic peanuts

(V)

serves 4
preparation 15 minutes
cooking 15–30 minutes

2 x 8 oz blocks firm tofu, drained
   and cut into cubes
all-purpose flour for dusting
canola or peanut oil for deep-frying

for the tomato sambal
1 tablespoon olive oil
1 lemon grass stalk, trimmed and
   finely chopped
1 red chili, sliced (seeded if
   you prefer)
1 garlic clove, crushed
1 tablespoon brown or palm sugar
4 tomatoes, roughly chopped
small handful of fresh cilantro,
   chopped
2 tablespoons ketjap manis or
   soy sauce
1 tablespoon prepared tamarind
   (from a jar)
4 tablespoons water
2 tablespoons crushed peanuts,
   to garnish

1 To make the sambal, heat the olive oil in a saucepan and fry the lemon grass, chili, and garlic for 1 minute. Remove from the heat and add all the remaining ingredients except the peanuts.

2 Toss the pieces of tofu in the flour. Pour enough oil into a wok or saucepan to cover the tofu and heat to 350–375°F, or until a cube of bread browns in 30 seconds. Add the tofu and fry until crisp and golden—this may take as long as 10 minutes—make sure it gets nice and crisp (do it in 2 batches if necessary). Drain on paper towels. Serve with the sambal spooned over and sprinkled with the crushed peanuts.

Deep-frying tofu makes it savory and crisp without being at all oily. Topped with a sweet and sour sambal, it makes an excellent first course or a light main course for 2 people.

sesame-roasted asparagus with wasabi vinaigrette

wasabi sesame oil

V

serves 4
preparation 10 minutes
cooking 15–20 minutes

1 lb asparagus, trimmed
2 tablespoons toasted sesame oil
salt

for the wasabi vinaigrette
1 packet (2 teaspoons) wasabi
   powder
2 tablespoons warm water
1 tablespoon rice vinegar
1 tablespoon flavorless vegetable
   oil such as grapeseed
2 tablespoons toasted sesame oil
salt and pepper, to taste

1 Toss the asparagus in the sesame oil, spread out on a baking sheet, and sprinkle with salt. Roast in a preheated oven, 425°F, for about 15 minutes, or until just tender and lightly browned in places.

2 To make the vinaigrette, put the wasabi into a lidded jar, add the warm water and mix to a paste. Add the rice vinegar, vegetable oil, sesame oil, and some salt and pepper, put the lid on and shake vigorously for a few seconds until smooth.

3 Arrange the asparagus on individual plates and drizzle the vinaigrette on top. Serve hot, warm, or cold.

If you can make the dressing in advance— 24 hours is not too long—the flavor of the wasabi mellows and is delicious and refreshing with the asparagus.

polenta fry stack with dipping sauces

lime avocado chili

(V)

serves 4
preparation 15 minutes–1 hour,
  depending on the type of
  polenta
cooking 30 minutes–1¼ hours,
  depending on the polenta

1 lb pack ready-made polenta
or
1 cup instant or traditional cornmeal
4 cups water
1 teaspoon salt
canola or peanut oil for deep-
  or pan-frying

for the dipping sauces
4 heaped tablespoons mayonnaise
1 tablespoon sun-dried tomato
  paste
7½ oz jar chunky salsa
1 large ripe avocado
3 tablespoons chopped cilantro
juice of 1 lime
pinch of chili powder
salt and pepper, to taste

1 If using ready-made polenta, blot with paper towels, then cut the polenta into chunky fries—a 1 lb block will make 24.

2 Or, if using instant cornmeal, make as directed on the package. For traditional cornmeal, heat the water and salt in a large saucepan. When the water comes to a boil, sprinkle the cornmeal over the surface, stirring all the time to prevent lumps. If you do get some lumps, whiz them away with an immersion blender or beater. Leave the mixture to simmer for 45 minutes, or until very thick, stirring from time to time.

3 Line an 7 x 11 inch jelly roll pan with nonstick parchment paper. Pour the cornmeal into the tin, spreading it to the edges and into the corners. Allow to cool and firm up.

4 Meanwhile, prepare the dipping sauces. Mix the mayonnaise with the tomato paste and put into a small bowl. Put the salsa into another bowl. Remove the pit and skin from the avocado and mash the flesh with the cilantro, lime juice, chili powder, and some salt and pepper to make a creamy, slightly chunky consistency. Put into a bowl.

5 Cut the firm cornmeal into fries about 6 inches long and ½ inch wide. Pour enough oil into a skillet to cover the polenta fries and heat to 350–375°F, or until a cube of bread browns in 30 seconds, then pan- or deep-fry them. It's easy to keep them separate if you pan-fry them, but make sure they're submerged in oil and cook them until they are really crisp and golden on one side, then turn them over and cook the other side thoroughly. Drain on paper towels. If you get them very crisp, the first batch will stay crisp while you cook the rest—keep them warm on paper towels in a cool oven.

6 Pile the polenta fries into a stack on a serving dish—or on individual plates—and serve with the 3 dipping sauces.

You can make these fries using ready-made polenta,
which makes them very quick and easy,
or you can make the polenta from scratch.

spicy thai noodles

ginger soy cilantro

serves 4
preparation 15 minutes
cooking 20 minutes

8 oz transparent (cellophane)
    noodles
2 tablespoons toasted sesame oil
2 teaspoons vegetarian Thai red
    curry paste
6 scallions, finely sliced
walnut-size piece of fresh ginger
    root, peeled and cut into
    thin shreds
2 garlic cloves, crushed
2–3 tablespoons rice vinegar
1–2 tablespoons shoyu or tamari
2 tablespoons chopped cilantro
salt and pepper, to taste

1 Put the noodles into a bowl, cover with boiling water and allow to stand for 5 minutes, then drain and toss in 1 tablespoon of the sesame oil to prevent the noodles from sticking together. Or follow the directions on the package.

2 Meanwhile, heat the rest of the sesame oil in a large saucepan, add the curry paste and let it sizzle for a few seconds. Add the scallions, ginger, and garlic and stir-fry for 1–2 minutes, to cook lightly.

3 Add the noodles to the pan and remove from the heat. Add the rice vinegar, shoyu or tamari, and some salt and pepper and toss lightly. Stir in the chopped cilantro and serve.

Cellophane noodles make a light and tasty accompaniment. If you can't get them, you could use other long, thin noodles for this recipe.

nut and miso pâté with cranberry relish and dill

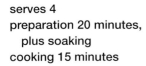

V

serves 4
preparation 20 minutes,
  plus soaking
cooking 15 minutes

½ cup cashew nuts
4 oz firm tofu, drained
1 garlic clove, crushed
4 teaspoons red miso
1 tablespoon nutritional yeast
  (see page 184) or a little yeast
  extract, to taste
1 teaspoon shoyu or tamari
4 teaspoons freshly squeezed
  lemon juice
white pepper
3 tablespoons chopped dill
4 sprigs of dill, to serve

for the cranberry relish
⅓ cup dried cranberries
⅔ cup full-bodied red wine
1 teaspoon olive oil
¼ teaspoon white mustard seeds
1 tablespoon finely chopped onion
1 garlic clove, finely chopped
1 teaspoon grated fresh ginger root
pinch of chili powder
1 tablespoon superfine sugar
1 tablespoon red wine vinegar
salt, to taste

1 First make the cranberry relish. Put the cranberries into a bowl, cover with the wine and set aside. Heat the olive oil in a small saucepan, add the mustard seeds, stir for a few seconds until they start to "pop," then add the onion, garlic, ginger, and chili powder. Cook over a gentle heat for about 5 minutes, or until the onion is tender.

2 Add the cranberries and their liquid to the pan, along with the sugar, red wine vinegar, and some salt. Bring to a boil, then reduce the heat and simmer, uncovered, for a few minutes, until the liquid has reduced and is syrupy and the cranberries are tender. Cool. (This will keep, covered, in the refrigerator for up to 2 weeks.)

3 For the pâté, cover the cashew nuts with cold water and allow to soak for 4–8 hours. Drain. Put into a food processor with the tofu, garlic, miso, yeast, shoyu or tamari, lemon juice, and a good pinch of white pepper and whiz to a very creamy pâté. Scrape into a bowl, cover and set aside until required.

4 To serve, stir the chopped dill and 4 tablespoons of the cranberry relish into the pâté. Arrange a spoonful in the center of each of 4 plates and garnish with a sprig of dill. Serve at once—the pâté loses its bright, fresh color if allowed to stand.

This wonderful and unusual pâté was inspired by a recipe that appeared in the *Vegetarian Times*. Serve with strips of warm pita bread.

braised whole baby carrots and fennel

fennel carrots parsley

(V)

serves 4
preparation 15 minutes
cooking 30 minutes

2 bunches 1½ lb baby carrots
3–4 baby fennel (about 14 oz)
4 tablespoons olive oil
4 garlic cloves, sliced
1¼ cups water
freshly squeezed lemon juice
salt and pepper, to taste
chopped parsley, to serve

1 If the carrots are really young, just scrub them; if they're older, peel them, but in either case keep them whole and leave ½ inch or so of the green stems attached at the top. If the fennel is really young and tender, just trim the tops.

2 Put the carrots and fennel into a saucepan with the olive oil, garlic, water, lemon juice, and some salt and pepper and bring to a boil. Reduce the heat, cover the pan and cook gently for about 30 minutes, checking occasionally to make sure they're not sticking. They're done when they feel very tender to the point of a knife, and the water has reduced to a syrupy golden glaze. Sprinkle with chopped parsley to serve.

These vegetables melt in your mouth and their golden liquid supplies a natural sauce for the dish. They are also very forgiving: they should be really tender, so it's almost impossible to overcook them, and they can be cooked in advance and gently reheated later if this is most convenient. If there are any left over, they also taste very good cold.

parsnips in sage butter

sage butter parsnips

serves 4
preparation 10 minutes
cooking 15 minutes

6–8 baby parsnips (about 1 lb)
2 tablespoons butter
1 tablespoon chopped sage
salt and pepper, to taste

1 Cut the parsnips lengthwise into quarters, to give long slim pieces. Put them into a saucepan with cold water to cover and bring to a boil, then reduce the heat and simmer for 10–15 minutes, or until tender.

2 Blend the butter with the sage and set aside.

3 Drain the parsnips and put into a warm serving dish, or return them to the saucepan. Season with salt and pepper, then add the sage butter and serve.

A simple yet wonderful combination of flavors.

cabbage with sesame and ginger

garlic cabbage sesame

(V)

serves 4
preparation 5 minutes
cooking 5 minutes

1 sweetheart or similar cabbage, shredded
1 tablespoon toasted sesame oil
1 tablespoon grated fresh ginger root
1 garlic clove, crushed
salt and pepper, to taste

1 Heat 1 inch of water in a saucepan, add the cabbage, cover with a lid and cook for about 5 minutes, or until the cabbage is tender. Drain.

2 Add the sesame oil, ginger, and garlic to the cabbage and stir well. Season with salt and pepper and serve at once.

This very simple treatment transforms cabbage.

It goes particularly well with Asian-style dishes.

saffron and garlic mash

serves 4
preparation 15 minutes,
   plus steeping
cooking 20 minutes

2¼ lb potatoes, peeled and cut
   into even-size pieces
⅔ cup light cream
good pinch of saffron threads
¼ cup butter
4 garlic cloves, crushed
salt and pepper, to taste

for the garnish
4 garlic cloves
1 tablespoon olive oil
1 tablespoon chopped parsley

1 Cover the potato pieces in boiling water and cook for about 20 minutes, or until tender.

2 Meanwhile, put the cream into a small saucepan with the saffron and bring almost to a boil, then remove from the heat, cover and allow to steep.

3 To prepare the garnish, cut the garlic cloves into thin slices. Heat the olive oil in a small pan, add the garlic and fry for a minute or so until the garlic is golden. Remove from the heat and set aside.

4 Drain the potatoes, reserving the water, then mash with the butter, crushed garlic, and saffron-infused cream (no need to remove the saffron threads) to make a smooth, creamy consistency. Add a small quantity of the reserved cooking water if needed. Season with salt and pepper.

5 Spoon the potato into a warmed serving dish, top with the fried pieces of garlic and the oil and some chopped parsley, and serve.

roast potatoes in sea salt and balsamic vinegar

(V)

serves 4
preparation 15 minutes
cooking 45 minutes

2 lb potatoes, peeled and cut into
   ½ inch chunks
canola or peanut oil for roasting
salt
balsamic vinegar

1 Put the potatoes into a saucepan, cover with water and bring to a boil, then reduce the heat and simmer for 7 minutes.

2 Pour ¼ inch of oil into a roasting pan large enough to hold the potatoes in a single layer, and put into a preheated oven, 400°F, until smoking hot.

3 Drain the potatoes and put them back into the saucepan, then put the lid on the pan and shake to roughen the outsides and make them cook more crisply.

4 Tip the potatoes into the hot oil and turn them with a large spoon so that the oil covers them all over. Roast for about 35 minutes, or until the potatoes are golden and crisp, turning them over when the undersides are done.

5 Using a draining spoon, transfer the potatoes to a warm serving dish. Sprinkle generously with salt, drizzle with balsamic vinegar, and serve.

Having tried various different oils for roasting potatoes, I've found that canola or peanut oil give the crispiest results.

dinners to dazzle

Vegetarian main courses often baffle

people, so here are nearly enough to have

a different one every day for four weeks.

Some are simple, some more complex,

some are in individual portions, others are

big, dramatic centerpieces; all, I hope, have

a bit of the "wow" factor.

red pepper, ricotta, and fennel tortellini with tarragon sauce

fennel cheese wine

serves 4
preparation 45 minutes,
   plus resting
cooking 30 minutes

for the pasta dough
3 cups white bread flour,
   preferably "00"
pinch of salt
3 eggs
1 tablespoon olive oil

for the filling
1 fennel bulb, trimmed
1 large red bell pepper, halved,
   cored, and seeded
1 garlic clove, crushed
½ cup ricotta cheese
1 cup freshly grated Parmesan-style
   cheese
salt and pepper, to taste

for the tarragon sauce
½ cup vegetable stock
   (use the fennel water)
½ cup dry white wine
2 cups heavy cream
2 good leafy sprigs of tarragon,
   chopped

1 To make the pasta dough, put the flour, salt, eggs, and olive oil into a food processor and whiz until combined. Gradually add enough cold water to make a soft, malleable dough—maybe 4–6 tablespoons. Remove from the food processor and knead on a lightly floured board for a few minutes until smooth, glossy, and pliable, then put into a plastic bag and allow to rest for 1 hour.

2 Meanwhile, make the filling. Run a potato peeler down the outside of the fennel to remove any potentially stringy bits. Quarter the fennel and cook in boiling water until tender—8–10 minutes. Strain—the water makes wonderful stock so save it for the sauce.

3 Broil the red pepper, cut-side down, under a hot broiler for about 10 minutes, or until black and blistered in places. Cool, then strip off the skin.

4 Chop the cooked fennel and red pepper finely. Add the garlic, ricotta, and Parmesan and season with salt and pepper. Divide into 20 equal portions.

5 To make the tortellini, divide the pasta dough into 20 equal portions. Take one portion and roll out on a floured board, making it as thin as you can—big enough to cut out 2 circles with a 2½ inch cutter. Continue with the rest of the dough, then take 2 of the circles and put a portion of filling in the center of one. Brush the edges with cold water and place the second circle on top, pressing down the edges well. Set aside and repeat the process with the rest of the circles and filling.

6 Bring a large saucepan of water to a boil. Drop in the tortellini and cook for about 6 minutes, or until the pasta is tender.

7 Meanwhile, to make the tarragon sauce, put the stock, wine, and cream into a saucepan and boil until reduced by half and slightly thickened. Remove from the heat, season, and add the tarragon.

8 Drain the pasta gently in a colander, then tip it onto a warmed dish, pour over the tarragon sauce and serve.

tagliatelle with leek and morel cream and crisp garlic

leeks garlic pasta

serves 4
preparation 20 minutes
cooking 30 minutes

12 oz dried tagliatelle
2 tablespoons olive oil
4 large garlic cloves, cut into thin
   slices, to serve

for the cream sauce
2 tablespoons butter
1 tablespoon olive oil
2½ cups roughly chopped morel
   mushrooms
2 garlic cloves, crushed
2½ cups cream—light, heavy, or
   a mixture
2 leeks, (about 8 oz) finely sliced
2 tablespoons chopped parsley
salt and pepper, to taste

1 To make the sauce, heat the butter and olive oil in a pan. Add the morels and crushed garlic and cook gently for 5–10 minutes, until any liquid they produce has boiled away. Pour in the cream and simmer, uncovered, until reduced by half.

2 Cook the leeks in boiling water to cover for 3–4 minutes, then drain (the water makes tasty stock) in a strainer and rinse under the cold tap to preserve the color. Drain well, then add to the cream mixture along with the parsley and some salt and pepper.

3 Bring a large saucepan of water to a boil, add the pasta and cook for 8–10 minutes, or as directed on the package. Drain into a colander and return to the hot saucepan with 1 tablespoon of the olive oil.

4 While the pasta is cooking, heat the remaining olive oil in a small skillet, add the sliced garlic and fry for a few seconds until golden and crisp—be careful not to let it burn and become bitter. Set aside.

5 Add the leek and morel sauce to the pasta in the pan and serve on warmed dishes, or serve the pasta first, then spoon the sauce on top. Either way, sprinkle with the garlic crisps and serve immediately.

rice noodles
with chili-ginger vegetables

noodles chilies soy

(V)

serves 4
preparation 30 minutes
cooking 20 minutes

for the noodles
8 oz rice noodles
1 tablespoon toasted sesame oil

for the sauce
1 tablespoon cornstarch
2 tablespoons shoyu or tamari
1 tablespoon superfine sugar
1 tablespoon toasted sesame oil
1 tablespoon mirin or dry sherry

for the chili-ginger vegetables
2 tablespoons flavorless oil,
  such as peanut, canola or
  grapeseed
2 tablespoons finely grated fresh
  ginger root
4 garlic cloves, crushed
1–2 large mild red chilies, seeded
  and finely sliced
1 head Chinese cabbage or 4 bok
  choy, sliced
4 cups bean sprouts
bunch of scallions, chopped
1¼ cups snow peas, halved
  lengthwise
1 red bell pepper, thinly sliced
8 oz can water chestnuts,
  drained and rinsed
bunch of fresh cilantro, chopped

1 Bring a large saucepan of water to a boil, drop in the rice noodles and cook for about 4 minutes, or as directed on the package, until al dente. Drain in a colander, then toss with the tablespoon of toasted sesame oil and set aside until required.

2 For the sauce, stir all the ingredients together and set aside.

3 Meanwhile, prepare the vegetables. Heat a large wok over a high flame until very hot. Add the oil, then throw in the ginger, garlic, and chilies. Let them sizzle, then add all the remaining ingredients except the cilantro and stir-fry over the heat for about 10 minutes, until all the vegetables are tender.

4 When the vegetables are tender, give the sauce a quick stir and pour into the pan, then stir for 1–2 minutes until the sauce has thickened and is coating the vegetables lightly. Season with salt.

4 Serve the noodles on a warm serving plate. Spoon the vegetables on top in a big, dramatic heap and scatter with the chopped cilantro. Serve at once.

You can do most of the preparation for this dish in advance and finish cooking and assembling it just before serving.

tea-smoked chestnut risotto

rice wine parmesan

serves 4
preparation 20 minutes,
** plus smoking**
cooking 35–40 minutes

for the tea-smoked chestnuts

½ cup uncooked rice
¼ cup dark brown sugar
3 tablespoons black tea leaves
1 tablespoon whole allspice
2 tablespoons molasses
1 cinnamon stick
2 x 7 oz vacuum packs
  whole peeled chestnuts

for the risotto

4 cups vegetable stock
1 tablespoon olive oil
2 onions, finely chopped
2 celery sticks, very finely chopped
2 garlic cloves, finely chopped
2 cups risotto rice
½ cup dry white wine
¼ cup butter
1 cup freshly grated Parmesan-style
  cheese
salt and pepper, to taste

1 Smoke the chestnuts an hour or so in advance. Line a wok with foil, then put in all the ingredients except the chestnuts and stir gently.

2 Arrange a rack over the wok and place the chestnuts on top. Cover with foil and cook over a medium heat for 10 minutes, then remove from the heat and allow to stand, covered, for another 10 minutes.

3 Meanwhile, make the risotto. Heat the stock, then reduce the heat and keep it hot over a very gentle heat.

4 Heat the olive oil in a large saucepan, add the onions and celery and stir, then cover and cook gently for 7–8 minutes, until tender but not browned. Stir in the garlic and cook for an additional minute or so.

5 Add the rice to the pan and stir over a gentle heat for 2–3 minutes, then pour in the wine and stir all the time as it bubbles away.

6 When the wine has disappeared, add a ladleful of the hot stock. Stir over a low-to-medium heat until the rice has absorbed the stock, then add another ladleful, and continue in this way until you've used up all the stock, the rice is tender and the consistency creamy—about 15–20 minutes.

7 Stir in the butter, chestnuts, and half the Parmesan, season with salt and pepper and serve, sprinkled with the rest of the cheese.

gateau of curried rice

cumin spinach onions

V

serves 4
preparation 1 hour
cooking 1 hour

for the rice

1¾ cups white basmati rice
1 teaspoon turmeric
3¾ cups water
2 tablespoons freshly squeezed
  lemon juice
salt and pepper, to taste

for the vegetable layers

3 onions, chopped
1 tablespoon olive oil
1 tablespoon grated fresh ginger
  root
4 garlic cloves, chopped
1 tablespoon cumin seeds
1 tablespoon coriander
2 teaspoons turmeric
1 small cauliflower, divided into
  small florets
⅔ cup water
½ cup cilantro
10 oz potatoes, peeled and cut
  into ½ inch dice
6 cups spinach
13 oz can chopped tomatoes
½ teaspoon dried red pepper flakes

1 Put the rice into a saucepan with the turmeric and water. Bring to a boil, then reduce the heat, cover the pan and cook very gently for 15 minutes, or until all the liquid has been absorbed. Remove from the heat and leave, still covered, for 5 minutes. Then add the lemon juice and stir gently with a fork—this will brighten the color of the rice. Season and set aside.

2 Fry the onions in the olive oil in a large saucepan for about 7 minutes, then stir in the ginger, garlic, cumin seeds, coriander, and turmeric and cook for an additional 2–3 minutes. Divide this mixture equally between 3 saucepans, to make the 3 fillings.

3 For the cauliflower filling, add the cauliflower to one of the saucepans and pour in the water. Bring to a boil, then reduce the heat, cover the pan and cook gently for about 10 minutes, or until the cauliflower is very tender and the water has disappeared. (Increase the heat and boil it off if it hasn't all gone.) Save some of the cilantro to garnish, chop the rest and add to the pan, then season with salt and pepper.

4 For the potato and spinach layer, add the potatoes to another of the saucepans. Cover and cook over a low heat for 10–15 minutes, until the potato is almost tender, adding a very little water if the mixture sticks. Add the spinach, cover and cook for about 10 minutes, or until the spinach is tender. Again, increase the heat and boil for 1–2 minutes if the spinach has produced a lot of liquid. Season.

5 For the tomato layer, add the tomatoes and chili flakes to the third saucepan and boil, uncovered, for 20–25 minutes, or until very thick. Season.

6 Line an 8 inch deep cake pan with nonstick paper to cover the base and sides. Put a quarter of the rice into the pan and spoon the cauliflower mixture on top, followed by another quarter of the rice, then the tomato mixture, more rice, the potato and spinach, and a final layer of rice. Press down firmly, cover with foil and cook in a preheated oven, 350°F, for about 20 minutes, or until heated through.

7 Turn out onto a warmed serving platter, strip off the paper, top with a sprig of cilantro and serve.

squash stuffed with moroccan rice

rice garlic spice

serves 4
preparation 20 minutes
cooking 30 minutes

2 small squash
1 garlic clove, crushed
olive oil for greasing
salt, to taste

for the rice filling
¾ cup white basmati rice
3 tablespoons raisins
1 tablespoon butter
1½ teaspoons ras el hanout
  (see page 184)
½ teaspoon turmeric
2 tablespoons lemon juice
8 green queen olives, pits
  removed, chopped
½ cup chopped cilantro

1 Cut the squash in half through their stems. Scoop out the seeds, then rub the cut surfaces of the squash with garlic and salt. Place cut-side down on a well-greased baking sheet and bake in a preheated oven, 400°F, for 30 minutes, or until the squash can easily be pierced with the point of a knife.

2 Meanwhile, make the rice filling. Bring half a saucepan of water to a boil, add the rice and bring back to a boil, then reduce the heat and simmer, uncovered, for 8–10 minutes, or until the rice is tender but still has some resistance.

3 Plump the raisins by soaking them in boiling water for 2–3 minutes.

4 Drain the rice. Reserve a couple of tablespoons for decoration. Return the rest to the pan with the butter, ras el hanout, turmeric, and lemon juice and mix well. Drain the raisins and add to the rice, along with the chopped olives and cilantro. Taste and season with salt.

5 Turn the squash so that they are cavity-side uppermost, then fill the cavities with the rice mixture, heaping it up. Serve immediately, or cover with foil and keep warm in the oven for a few minutes before serving.

Mini squash can be used, but they need to be large enough to be baked in halves and then stuffed, because that way they cook really well.

celeriac rosti with green beans
in almond butter

almonds beans oil

(V)

serves 4
preparation 30 minutes
cooking 20 minutes

1 celeriac, about 1 lb 10 oz,
   peeled and grated
1 cup slivered almonds
2–4 tablespoons olive oil
salt and pepper, to taste

for the beans
1¾ cups slim green beans,
   lightly trimmed and cut in half
4 teaspoons roasted almond butter
   (see page 184)

1 Mix the celeriac with the almonds and some salt and pepper.

2 Heat 2 tablespoons of the olive oil in a skillet large enough to hold 4 x 8 inch metal chef's rings—or you may need to use 2 skillets. Place the rings in the skillet or skillets and fill with the celeriac mixture, dividing it evenly between them and pressing down well. Cover with a plate or lid and cook over a gentle heat for about 10 minutes, or until the underside is golden brown.

3 Using a spatula, flip each rosti over (still in its ring) and press down the mixture so that it is touching the surface of the skillet. Cover as before and cook the second side.

4 Bring 1 inch of water to a boil in a saucepan, add the green beans and cook for 3–4 minutes, or until just tender. Drain, return to the pan and toss with the almond butter and some salt and pepper.

5 Place a celeriac rosti on each plate and top with green beans. Slip off the rings and serve.

chickpea flatcake topped with lemon- and honey-roasted vegetables

cumin honey lemon

serves 4–6
preparation 30 minutes
cooking 45 minutes

4 tablespoons olive oil
3 large onions, finely chopped
3 large garlic cloves, crushed
2 teaspoons cumin seeds
3 x 13 oz cans chickpeas,
    drained and rinsed
salt and pepper, to taste
lemon wedges and sprig of flat leaf
    parsley, to garnish

for the roasted vegetables
1 lb 12 oz Jerusalem artichokes,
    peeled and cut into 1 inch chunks
14 oz carrots, scraped and cut
    into batons
3 tablespoons olive oil
3 tablespoons honey
3 tablespoons freshly squeezed
    lemon juice
grated zest of 1 lemon

1 Start with the roasted vegetables. Put the artichokes and carrots into a roasting dish with the olive oil, honey, lemon juice and zest, and some salt and pepper and mix gently. Then roast in a preheated oven, 350°F, for about 45 minutes, turning the vegetables occasionally.

2 Next, make the flatcake. Heat 2 tablespoons of the olive oil in a saucepan, add the onions and cover and fry gently for 10 minutes. Add the garlic and cumin seeds and cook for an additional 2–3 minutes. Remove from the heat and add the chickpeas and some salt and pepper. Mash the mixture thoroughly.

3 Put the mixture into a lightly greased 12 inch round removable-based tart pan and smooth the top. Cover with foil and bake for 15 minutes, remove the foil, pour the remaining olive oil over the top and bake for an additional 5–10 minutes, until golden—don't let it get dry. Remove from the oven. Turn the flatcake out of the pan and slide it onto a warm serving dish. Spoon the roasted vegetables on top, garnish with lemon wedges and a sprig of flat leaf parsley and serve.

dauphinoise roulade
with red chard and dolcelatte filling

cheese potatoes chard

serves 4
preparation 40 minutes
cooking 45 minutes

for the roulade
olive oil for greasing and brushing
1 lb 13 oz potatoes, peeled and
    thinly sliced
1 garlic clove, crushed
salt and pepper, to taste
green salad, to serve

for the filling
1 lb red chard, leaves and
    stems separated
6 oz dolcelatte cheese

1 Line an 8½ x 12½ inch jelly roll pan with nonstick paper and brush with olive oil. Mix the potatoes with the garlic and some salt and pepper, arrange them carefully and evenly in the pan and brush with olive oil. Cover with a piece of nonstick paper and bake in a preheated oven, 400°F, for 30 minutes, then remove the paper and bake for an additional 5–10 minutes, until the potatoes are tender and golden brown. Cool and set aside.

2 Chop the chard stems and boil in water to soften for 5 minutes, then add the leaves, cover the pan and cook for 7–10 minutes until tender. Drain very well, then mix with the dolcelatte.

3 Turn the roulade out onto its covering piece of nonstick paper. Cover the surface with the chard mixture. Starting with one of the short edges, carefully roll up the roulade, using the paper underneath to help—it rolls up quite easily and you can be firm with it!

4 Put the roulade onto a heatproof serving dish. About 15 minutes before you want to serve it, pop the roulade back into the oven, uncovered, until heated through and crisp and golden on the outside. Serve at once, with a green salad.

This wonderful, unusual roulade can be made in advance, ready for reheating just before serving, when it will become crisp and gorgeous. A tomato sauce, such as the one on page 28, and fine green beans go well with it.

bubble-and-squeak cakes
with beet relish

honey cabbage onion

serves 4
preparation 20 minutes,
**   plus standing**
cooking 30 minutes

2 lb potatoes, peeled and cut into
    even-size pieces
3 tablespoons butter
1 sweetheart or similar cabbage,
    shredded
6 scallions, finely chopped
2–3 tablespoons wholewheat flour
olive oil for pan-frying
salt and pepper, to taste
drizzle of olive oil and sprigs of dill,
    to garnish

for the beet relish
2 cooked beets, peeled and diced
2 tablespoons finely chopped onion
1 tablespoon honey
1 tablespoon cider vinegar

1 First make the relish. Put the beet into a bowl, stir in the onion, honey, and cider vinegar and season with salt and pepper. Set aside for at least 30 minutes until needed—this relish improves with keeping: it's fine to make it several hours in advance if convenient.

2 Meanwhile, cover the potatoes in boiling water and cook for about 20 minutes, or until tender. Drain and mash with the butter.

3 Put the cabbage into 1 inch of boiling water, cover and cook until tender—about 6 minutes. Drain well, then add the cabbage to the potatoes, along with the scallions and some salt and pepper.

4 Form the mixture into 4 large flat cakes. Just before you want to serve the cakes, coat them all over in flour, then immediately pan-fry in sizzling hot olive oil until browned and crisp on both sides, flipping them over to cook the second side.

5 Serve at once, topping each one with a spoonful of beet relish, a drizzle of oil, and sprigs of dill.

Sometimes the simplest things are best!
I don't know what it is about these, but
everyone loves them.

ricotta and plum tomato cake with pesto sauce

eggs tomatoes basil

serves 4
preparation 20 minutes
cooking 1¼ hours

4½ cups ricotta cheese
2⅓ finely grated Parmesan-style
    cheese
¼ cup butter, melted
2 eggs plus 2 egg yolks
2 large plum tomatoes, about 8 oz,
    sliced into rounds
bunch of basil, torn
salt and pepper, to taste
¼ cup toasted pine nuts and
    basil leaves, to garnish

for the sauce
4 tablespoons pesto
4 tablespoons water

1 Put the ricotta, Parmesan, butter, whole eggs, and egg yolks into a food processor and whiz to a smooth cream. Season with salt and pepper.

2 Spoon half the ricotta mixture into the base of an 8½ inch springform pan. Arrange the tomatoes on top and scatter with torn basil and some salt and pepper. Gently spoon the rest of the ricotta mixture on top.

3 Bake in a preheated oven, 375°F, for 1–1¼ hours, or until risen and lightly browned, firm to touch and a toothpick inserted into the center comes out clean—cover the top lightly with a piece of foil if it starts to get too brown.

4 Remove from the oven and allow to stand for 5 minutes to settle, then remove the sides of the pan and put the cake onto a warm serving dish.

5 To make the sauce, mix the pesto and water. Drizzle some of this over the top of the cake and serve the rest in a small bowl. Sprinkle the top of the cake with pine nuts and basil leaves and serve at once.

refritos gateau

beans avocado cream

serves 4
preparation 20 minutes
cooking 35–40 minutes

2 onions, chopped
2 tablespoons olive oil
1 green chili, seeded and chopped
4 garlic cloves, crushed
4 x 14 oz cans red kidney beans,
    drained and rinsed
4 tablespoons tomato paste
2 eggs
salt and pepper, to taste

to assemble and garnish
7½ oz jar tomato salsa
1⅓ cups grated cheddar cheese
1 large avocado
1 cup sour cream
a little chopped red sweet pepper
1–2 tablespoons chopped cilantro
3½ oz package plain tortilla chips

1 Fry the onions in the olive oil in a large saucepan for about 10 minutes. Add the green chili and garlic and cook for an additional 1–2 minutes.

2 Remove from the heat and add the beans, mashing them to make a chunky mixture that holds together. Stir in the tomato paste and eggs and season with salt and pepper.

3 Line 2 x 8 inch round removable-based pans with nonstick paper. Divide the mixture between them and bake in a preheated oven, 350°F, for 25 minutes, or until firm in the center.

4 Turn one of the bean cakes out onto an ovenproof plate and strip off the lining paper. Spread about 4 tablespoons of the salsa on top, then cover with the cheddar. Turn out the second bean cake, strip off the lining paper and place the cake on top of the cheese, pressing down firmly but gently. If not serving immediately, cover with foil and place in the oven until just before you want to serve it—the cheese layer will melt a bit.

5 To serve, peel the avocado and cut into long slices. Cover the top of the cake with sour cream, letting it drizzle down the sides. Arrange the slices of avocado on the cream and scatter with chopped red pepper and cilantro. Stick a few tortilla chips jauntily in the top (serve the rest in a bowl) and serve at once.

A gateau of refritos—Mexican refried beans—makes a luscious and dramatic centerpiece dish.

bean, beer, and vegetable puff pie

leeks celery pastry

serves 4
preparation 30 minutes,
**   plus cooling**
cooking 1 hour

2 tablespoons olive oil
2 onions, finely chopped
2 celery sticks, sliced
3 garlic cloves, chopped
1½ tablespoons all-purpose
    white flour
1¼ cups vegetable stock
⅔ cup beer
1 tablespoon shoyu or tamari
2 teaspoons prepared mustard
1 lb carrots, sliced
1 lb leeks, cut into 1 inch lengths
8 oz baby onions, halved
    or quartered
14 oz can lima beans, drained
    and rinsed
1–2 tablespoons superfine sugar
12 oz frozen ready-rolled all-butter
    puff pastry (see page 184)
salt and pepper, to taste

1 Heat the olive oil in a large saucepan, add the chopped onions and celery and stir, then cover and allow to cook gently for 7–8 minutes, until tender but not browned. Stir in the garlic and cook for an additional minute or so.

2 Sprinkle in the flour and stir over the heat for 1–2 minutes until the flour turns nut-brown. Pour in the stock and beer and stir over the heat until the mixture has thickened slightly.

3 Stir in the shoyu or tamari, the mustard, and some salt and pepper, then add the carrots, leeks, and baby onions. Bring to a boil, then reduce the heat, cover the pan and cook gently for about 25 minutes, or until the vegetables are tender. Add the lima beans and sugar and season with salt and pepper, then set aside to cool.

4 Transfer the vegetable mixture to a shallow pie dish. Measure the pastry against the dish, cut off the excess and cut this into long thin strips. Brush the rim of the pie dish and the long strips of pastry with a little cold water. Press the strips all round the rim of the dish. Ease the pastry on top of the pie, so that it rests on the pastry-covered rim of the dish. Press the edges of the pastry, decorate as desired and make a steam-hole in the center.

5 Bake the pie in a preheated oven, 400°F, for 20 minutes, or until the pastry is puffy and golden brown. Serve at once.

This old-fashioned homely dish goes well with mashed potatoes and a cooked green vegetable, such as cabbage or Brussels sprouts.

stilton, apple, and sage crêpes with berry sauce

apples port stilton

serves 4
preparation 30 minutes
cooking 30 minutes

8 oz shallots, chopped
1 tablespoon olive oil
12 oz apples, peeled and chopped
1 cup fine fresh white bread crumbs
5 oz Stilton cheese, crumbled
1 tablespoon chopped sage
8 crêpes, made according to the
   pancake recipe on page 158,
   omitting sugar, or store-bought
   crêpes
2 eggs, beaten
cornmeal for coating
canola or peanut oil for deep-frying
salt and pepper, to taste
red chard leaves, to garnish

for the blackberry sauce
4 tablespoons blackberry jelly or
   preserve
1 teaspoon Dijon mustard
2 tablespoons each freshly squeezed
   orange and lemon juice
4 tablespoons port

1 Fry the shallots in the olive oil for 5 minutes, then add the apples, cover and cook for an additional 5–10 minutes, or until the shallots and apples are tender. Remove from the heat and add the bread crumbs, Stilton, and sage, then season with salt and pepper.

2 Put a spoonful of the filling toward the edge of a crêpe. Fold the sides over it and roll up, as if wrapping a parcel. Continue until all the crêpes and filling are used. Carefully dip each crêpe in beaten egg, then into cornmeal, to coat completely. Put the coated crêpes on a piece of nonstick paper and chill until required.

3 To make the sauce, mix all the ingredients in a small saucepan and simmer over a moderate heat for 4–5 minutes until glossy and syrupy. Pour into a sauce boat to serve.

4 Heat the oil to 350–375°F, or until a cube of bread browns in 30 seconds. Deep-fry the crêpes until crisp and golden brown, then drain on paper towels. To serve, pour a little sauce on each plate, add a crêpe or 2 and garnish with a red chard leaf.

brie and cranberry soufflés

cheddar brie eggs

serves 4
preparation 30 minutes
cooking 40 minutes

for the cranberry sauce
1½ cups cranberries
½ cup superfine sugar

for the soufflés
1 tablespoon butter, plus extra
  for greasing the dish
1 tablespoon all-purpose white flour
½ cup milk
1 teaspoon Dijon mustard
⅓ cup grated cheddar cheese
pinch of white pepper
3 egg whites
2 egg yolks
4 oz Brie cheese, not too ripe,
  thinly sliced
salt, to taste

1 First make the cranberry sauce. Wash the cranberries and put them, with just the water clinging to them, into a saucepan and heat gently for 10 minutes, or until they're soft. Add the sugar and simmer gently for about 15 minutes, or until "jelly-like." Set aside.

2 Melt the butter in a saucepan and stir in the flour. Cook for a minute, stirring, then remove from the heat and gradually stir in the milk. Bring to a boil and cook, stirring, until the sauce thickens, then remove from the heat and stir in the mustard, cheddar, white pepper, and a little salt. Allow to cool slightly.

3 Beat the egg whites until they stand in soft peaks. Stir the egg yolks into the cheese mixture, then stir in 1 tablespoon of the beaten whites to loosen the mixture. Gently fold in the rest of the egg whites.

4 Generously grease 4 x ⅓ cup ramekins or individual soufflé dishes. Put 1 tablespoon of the mixture into each dish, then cover with 1–2 slices of Brie and 1–2 teaspoons of the cranberry sauce. Spoon the rest of the soufflé mixture on top—it can come to the top of the dishes but no higher.

5 Stand the dishes in a roasting pan, pour in boiling water to come halfway up the sides and bake in a preheated oven, 350°F, for 13–15 minutes until risen and golden brown and a toothpick inserted into the center of a soufflé comes out clean. Serve at once.

You won't need the full quantity of cranberry sauce for this, but it's not worth making less— serve the remainder with the soufflés, or keep it in a jar in the refrigerator for up to 4 weeks.

individual pea, spinach, and mint pithiviers

spinach cream pastry

serves 4
preparation 25 minutes
cooking 30 minutes

6 cups baby spinach leaves
2 cups frozen petit pois, thawed
4 tablespoons chopped mint
12 oz frozen ready-rolled all-butter
  puff pastry (see page 184)
7 oz Boursin garlic and herb
  cream cheese
4 tablespoons cream, to glaze
salt and pepper, to taste

1 Cook the spinach in a dry saucepan for 1–2 minutes until wilted, then drain and cool. Season with salt and pepper. Mash the peas with the mint—give them a quick whiz in a food processor or with an immersion blender—so they hold together a bit.

2 Lay the pastry on a board and roll to make it even thinner, then cut into 4 x 4 inch circles for the bases, and 4 slightly larger ones, about 6¾ inch (a saucer is useful for cutting round) to go over the top.

3 Place the smaller circles on a cookie sheet. Put a layer of spinach on top of each circle, leaving about ½ inch free round the edges. Put a quarter of the Boursin on top of the spinach, then heap the peas on top and around the Boursin. Cover with the remaining pastry circles, pressing the edges neatly together and crimping with your fingers or the prongs of a fork. Make a hole in the center of each and decorate the top with little cuts spiraling out from the center, like a traditional pithiviers, if you desire. All this can be done in advance. When ready to cook, brush the tops with the cream.

4 Bake the pithiviers in a preheated oven, 400°F, for about 25 minutes, or until puffed up, golden brown, and crisp. Serve at once.

wild mushroom tempura with garlic mayonnaise

(V)

serves 4
preparation 15 minutes
cooking 30 minutes

1 lb mixed wild mushrooms, torn
  into bite-size pieces
canola or peanut oil, for deep-frying
garlic mayonnaise or aioli, to serve

for the tempura batter
1 cup all-purpose white flour
1⅓ cups cornstarch
3 teaspoons baking powder
¾ cup sparkling water
salt, to taste

1 Just before you want to serve the mushrooms, heat sufficient oil for deep-frying in a deep-fat fryer to 350–375°F, or until a cube of bread browns in 30 seconds.

2 While the oil is heating, make the batter. Put the flour, cornstarch, and baking powder into a bowl with some salt. Pour in the water and stir the mixture quickly with a fork or chopstick to make a batter.

3 Dip pieces of mushroom into the batter, then put them into the hot oil for 1–2 minutes until they are golden brown and very crisp. Lift them out onto paper towels. You will need to do a number of batches, but the first ones will keep crisp while you do the rest.

4 Pile the tempura on a plate and serve immediately with the garlic mayonnaise or aioli.

Provided you buy a vegan mayonnaise, this makes a luxurious vegan main course—the unusual tempura batter is light and very crisp. A bag of mixed wild mushrooms from a supermarket is perfect for this recipe.

portobello steaks en croûte

brandy garlic cream

serves 4
preparation 10 minutes
cooking 25 minutes

4 portobello mushrooms
4 garlic cloves, chopped
4 teaspoons brandy
3½ oz jar vegetarian tapenade,
  green or black
12 oz frozen ready-rolled all-butter
  puff pastry (see page 184)
4–6 tablespoons cream or soya
  cream, to glaze
salt and pepper, to taste

1 Sit the mushrooms stem-side up and make crisscross cuts all over the stem-tops and surface, being careful not to cut right through the base of the mushroom.

2 Rub the garlic into the cuts, along with the brandy and some salt and pepper, then top each with a generous amount of tapenade, dividing the jar between them.

3 Spread out the pastry on a floured board and roll it a bit to make it as thin as you can. Cut it into 4 pieces—they will be roughly square.

4 Put a mushroom stem-side up into the center of each pastry square and fold the sides up to encase it, but not completely cover the top. Put the mushroom parcels onto a baking sheet and brush the sides and top of the pastry with cream.

5 Bake in a preheated oven, 400°F, for 25 minutes, or until the pastry is puffed up and golden brown and the mushrooms are tender.

Braised Whole Baby Carrots and Fennel (see page 44) together with Saffron and Garlic Mash (see page 47) would go well with this.

eggplant schnitzels with watercress sauce

arame tofu cream

(V)

serves 4
**preparation 30 minutes, plus
   soaking**
cooking 25 minutes

¼ oz arame seaweed
2 eggplants, stems trimmed
olive oil for brushing and pan-frying
7½ oz block smoked tofu, drained
6 tablespoons cornstarch
5 tablespoons water
⅛ cup dried bread crumbs
salt and pepper, to taste
lemon slices, to serve

for the watercress sauce
bunch or package of watercress
¾ cup light cream or unsweetened
   soya cream
1 teaspoon cornstarch

1 Cover the arame with cold water and allow to soak for 10 minutes.

2 Meanwhile, cut the eggplants lengthwise into 4 slices—or in half, then in half again. (Two of the slices will have skin on one side.) Brush the cut surfaces of the eggplant with olive oil, place on a broiler pan and cook under a hot broiler until they are lightly browned and feel tender to the point of a knife, turning them over when the first side is done.

3 Whiz the tofu and arame to a puree in a food processor or using an immersion blender. Season with salt and pepper, then spread some of the mixture thickly on one slice of eggplant and press another slice on top to make a fat sandwich. Repeat with all the slices, dividing the tofu mixture evenly between them.

4 Put the cornstarch into a bowl and mix in the water to make a thick coating paste. Dip each eggplant sandwich into the paste, then into the bread crumbs, making sure it's thoroughly coated. Pan-fry the schnitzels on both sides in hot olive oil, drain on paper towels and serve garnished with slices of lemon and accompanied by the watercress sauce.

5 To make the sauce, whiz the watercress, cream, and cornstarch to a puree in a food processor or using an immersion blender. Heat gently, stirring, until thickened.

Thick slices of broiled eggplant sandwiched with smoked tofu and arame—a delicately flavored seaweed—give these schnitzels a gorgeous juiciness and smoky flavor, encased in a crisp crumb coating.

lemon-glazed and seared halloumi with herb salad

honey herbs lemon

serves 4
preparation 10 minutes,
   plus marinating
cooking 5–10 minutes

2 x 8 oz packages halloumi cheese,
   drained
4 tablespoons freshly squeezed
   lemon juice
2 tablespoons honey

for the herb salad
6 cups mixed baby leaf and
   herb salad
2 tablespoons olive oil
salt and pepper, to taste

1 Cut the halloumi into slices about ¼ inch thick. Put them on a plate in a single layer.

2 Mix the lemon juice with the honey and pour over the halloumi, turning it to coat the slices all over. Set aside for at least 1 hour.

3 When you are ready to serve, toss the leaves with the olive oil and some salt and pepper and divide between 4 plates.

4 Put the slices of halloumi into a dry skillet over a moderate heat, reserving any liquid. Fry on one side until golden brown, then flip them over and fry the second side. This is a very quick process as they cook fast. When the second sides are done, pour in any liquid that was left and let it bubble up until it has mostly evaporated and becomes a sweet glaze.

5 Arrange the slices of halloumi on top of the salad and serve at once.

The halloumi can be marinated well in advance, but cook it quickly at the last minute so that it is light and delicious.

lentil cakes in citrus broth

lime lentils onion

(V)

serves 4
preparation 1 hour
cooking 45–50 minutes

for the lentil cakes
1½ cups Puy lentils
1 onion, roughly chopped
3¾ cups water
½ cup packet chopped cilantro
1 tablespoon coriander
juice of 1½ limes
olive oil for pan-frying
salt and pepper, to taste

for the broth
2½ cups vegetable stock
2 lemon grass stalks, crushed
green tops from a bunch of scallions
3–4 kaffir lime leaves
2 garlic cloves
½ cup chopped cilantro

1 Put the lentils into a saucepan with the onion and water. Bring to a boil, then reduce the heat, cover the pan and simmer very gently for 40–45 minutes, or until the lentils are very tender and all the water has been absorbed. Add a little more water toward the end of cooking if the lentils are sticking, but make sure no water remains.

2 Mash the lentils with the cilantro and coriander, the lime juice, and some salt and pepper. Form into 12 cakes, pressing the mixture so it holds together. Fry the lentil cakes in a little hot olive oil until crisp and browned on both sides.

3 To make the broth, put the stock into a saucepan with the lemon grass, scallion tops, lime leaves, and garlic. Bring to a boil, then reduce the heat and simmer, uncovered, for a few minutes, until the liquid has reduced by half. Strain, discard the flavorings and return the stock to the pan with the chopped cilantro.

4 Serve the lentil cakes in shallow bowls in a pool of the broth. Cabbage with Sesame and Ginger (see page 46) would go well with this.

carrot, parsnip, and chestnut terrine with red wine gravy

fennel eggs wine

serves 4
preparation 30 minutes
cooking 1 hour 5 minutes

3 garlic cloves, chopped
¼ cup butter
2 tablespoons dried bread crumbs
2 tablespoons olive oil
2 onions, chopped
1 cup parsnips, cut into
    ½ inch chunks
1 cup carrots, sliced into rounds
2 cups chopped fennel
1 teaspoon caraway seeds
7 oz vacuum pack whole
    peeled chestnuts
1½ cups fine soft wholewheat
    bread crumbs
4 tablespoons lemon juice
2 tablespoons shoyu or tamari
3 eggs, beaten
2 tablespoons chopped parsley
salt and pepper, to taste

for the red wine gravy
2 onions, finely chopped
1 tablespoon olive oil
2 tablespoons all-purpose
    white flour
¾ cup vegetable stock
¾ cup red wine
2 tablespoons shoyu or tamari
sugar, to taste

1 Line a 1 lb 12 oz loaf pan with a strip of nonstick paper. Mix the garlic with the butter and use half of this to grease the lined base and sides of the pan, then coat the base and sides with half the dried bread crumbs.

2 Heat the olive oil in a large saucepan and add the onions, parsnips, carrots, and fennel. Cover and cook very gently for about 20 minutes, stirring from time to time, or until all the vegetables are tender.

3 Add the caraway seeds and cook for 1–2 minutes longer, then remove from the heat and mix in the chestnuts, soft breadcrumbs, lemon juice, shoyu or tamari, the eggs, parsley, and some salt and pepper.

4 Spoon the mixture into the prepared loaf pan and level the surface. Sprinkle the top with the rest of the dried bread crumbs and dot with the remaining garlic butter. Bake in a preheated oven, 350°F, for 40 minutes, until firm on top and a toothpick inserted into the center comes out clean.

5 While the loaf is cooking, make the gravy. Fry the onions in the olive oil for 10 minutes, until they are tender and lightly browned. Add the flour and stir over the heat for 3–4 minutes, until nut-brown—the mixture will be very dry. Stir in the stock and wine, then simmer over a moderate heat until thickened. Add the shoyu or tamari and season with salt, pepper, and perhaps a touch of sugar. Serve as it is or, if you prefer smooth gravy, pass it through a strainer. Either way, add more stock if you want it thinner.

6 Serve the terrine in thick slices with the red wine gravy.

toover dhal with lime and cilantro leaf dumplings

cloves cumin lime

serves 4
preparation 20 minutes
cooking 1¼ hours

for the dhal
1½ cups toover (toor) dhal
   (see page 185), thoroughly
   washed in hot water and drained
8 cups water
2 tablespoons olive oil
2 whole cloves
1 cinnamon stick
1–2 dried red chilies
6 dried kaffir lime leaves
1 whole green chili
13 oz can chopped tomatoes
1 tablespoon garam masala
1 tablespoon freshly squeezed
   lemon juice
sugar, salt, and pepper, to taste

for the cilantro dumplings
1 cup self-rising flour
2 teaspoons cumin seeds
½ cup chopped cilantro
finely grated zest of 1 lime
4 tablespoons olive oil
4 tablespoons water

1 Put the toover dhal into a large saucepan with the water and bring to a boil. Using a perforated spoon, scoop off the foam, then reduce the heat, cover the pan and allow to cook very gently for about 1 hour, until very soft.

2 Meanwhile, heat the olive oil in a medium saucepan and add the cloves, cinnamon stick, and dried chilies. Let them sizzle for about half a minute, then add the lime leaves and sizzle again. Stir in the green chili, cook for a few more seconds, then add the tomatoes. Bring to a boil, then reduce the heat and allow to simmer, uncovered, for 15–20 minutes, or until very thick, stirring often to prevent sticking. Remove the cinnamon stick, chili and any large pieces of lime leaf.

3 Stir the dhal to give a creamy consistency, then add the tomato mixture, garam masala, lemon juice, ½–1 tablespoon sugar, and some salt and pepper.

4 To make the dumplings, put the flour into a bowl, add all the remaining ingredients with salt to taste, and mix quickly to a soft dough. Form into 8 dumplings. Bring the dhal to a gentle boil and drop in the dumplings. Reduce the heat, cover the pan and cook for about 15 minutes, or until the dumplings have risen to the surface and are cooked inside. Serve from the pot or carefully transfer to a warmed casserole.

The dumplings are very British, but with the fresh Asian flavorings they seem made to go with this dish perfectly.

decadent desserts and cakes

For a special, memorable meal, a gorgeous

pudding or cake reawakens people's interest

after the delights of the main course and

provides the final drama. Here is a varied

selection of delights for your "closing act,"

designed to satisfy all tastes and, who knows,

even evoke a round of applause …

melting chocolate puddings

vanilla eggs cocoa

serves 4
preparation 25 minutes
cooking 20 minutes

¼ cup butter, plus extra for greasing
4 oz bittersweet chocolate, broken
2 eggs
¼ cup superfine sugar
½ teaspoon vanilla extract
1 tablespoon all-purpose white flour
8 squares, 1–2 oz good-quality
    white chocolate
cocoa powder for dusting
thick cream, to serve

1 Line 4 x ⅔ cup individual metal pudding basins with a disk of nonstick paper in the base and butter them very thoroughly.

2 Put the dark chocolate and butter into a heatproof bowl set over a pan of gently steaming water and allow to melt, then stir, remove from the heat and allow to cool slightly.

3 Using an electric beater, beat together the eggs, sugar, and vanilla extract until very thick and pale—this takes at least 5 minutes.

4 Gently fold the melted chocolate and flour into the beaten mixture until completely incorporated. Put 1 tablespoon of the chocolate mixture into each pudding basin and put them into a preheated oven, 400°F, for 5 minutes, then remove them and quickly fill the basins with the rest of the mixture. Drop 2 squares of the white chocolate into each. Put them back into the oven and bake for 11–12 minutes, or until risen and a bit crusty around the edges.

5 Remove from the oven and allow to stand for 1–2 minutes, then slip a knife around the sides and invert each pudding over a warmed plate. Leave for another 30 seconds, then gently lift off the pudding basins. Dust the puddings with a little cocoa powder and serve immediately with thick cream.

Little melting chocolate puddings have become a modern classic—and these provide a new twist because when you cut them open, white chocolate oozes out! They are easy to do and can be prepared well in advance, ready for cooking just before serving.

little plum upside-down puddings
with cinnamon custard

plums sugar milk

serves 4
preparation 30 minutes
cooking 30 minutes

butter, for greasing
½ cup superfine sugar, plus more
    as required
1 lb plums, sliced and pits removed
4 tablespoons water

for the spongecake
2 eggs
¼ cup superfine sugar
½ cup self-rising flour

for the custard
2 egg yolks
1 teaspoon cornstarch
1 tablespoon superfine sugar
1¼ cups whole milk
½ cinnamon stick

1 Line a baking sheet with nonstick paper, grease generously with butter and place 4 inch chefs' rings on it. Sprinkle inside the rings lightly with some of the sugar.

2 Put the plums into a saucepan with the rest of the sugar and the water. Cover and cook over a moderate heat for 3–4 minutes, or until the plums are just tender but not collapsed. Remove from the heat. Taste and add more sugar if necessary.

3 To make the spongecake, beat the eggs and sugar together until very thick and pale—this takes about 5 minutes with an electric beater. Sift the flour over the top and fold in gently with a spatula.

4 Divide the plums between the rings, spreading them out so that they cover the whole area. Spoon the spongecake mixture on top, leveling it off. Bake in a preheated oven, 350°F, for 20 minutes, or until the cake springs back when touched lightly in the center.

5 To make the custard, put the egg yolks, cornstarch and sugar into a bowl and beat together. Pour the milk into a saucepan, add the cinnamon stick and bring to a boil. Gradually beat the hot milk into the egg mixture, then return the mixture to the pan and stir over a gentle heat for a few minutes until the mixture thickens and will coat the back of a spoon. Remove the cinnamon stick. The custard can be served hot or cold.

6 Run a knife around the edges of the rings, then turn each pudding out onto a warmed serving plate. Pour a little of the custard around, and serve the rest in a pitcher.

Chefs' rings are ideal for making these, but if you don't have any, you could use 4 inch removable-based shallow tart pans lined with a circle of nonstick paper.

pear and brioche charlotte

vanilla pears butter

serves 4
preparation 25 minutes
cooking 1¼ hours

1½ lb pears, peeled, cored, and
    cut into pieces
2 tablespoons superfine sugar
2 tablespoons water
1 vanilla bean
8–10 slices of brioche
½ cup butter, melted
1 cup mascarpone cheese
2 egg yolks
2 tablespoons raw sugar
thick pouring cream, to serve
    (optional)

1 Put the pears into a saucepan with the superfine sugar, water, and vanilla bean. Bring to a boil, then reduce the heat, cover the pan and allow to cook very gently for about 30 minutes, or until the pears are very tender. Set aside until completely cold.

2 Brush the slices of brioche with the melted butter and arrange them in an 8 inch sponge layer cake pan with a removable base, or a shallow ovenproof casserole, covering the base and sides and saving some slices for the top.

3 Beat the mascarpone a little to soften. Mix in the egg yolks and the pears together with any liquid. Spoon this on top of the brioche, then put the remaining brioche slices on top, brush with melted butter and sprinkle with raw sugar.

4 Bake in a preheated oven, 350°F, for about 40 minutes, or until the charlotte is golden, crisp and set in the middle—cover it with a piece of foil toward the end of the cooking time if it seems to be getting too crisp on top before the inside is set.

5 Serve hot, warm, or cold, with pouring cream, if you desire.

banana and earl grey cake

tea eggs banana

serves 4
preparation 10 minutes,
   plus standing for the tea
cooking 30–35 minutes

8 Earl Grey tea bags
1 cup boiling water
1 large banana
½ cup soft butter
½ cup soft brown sugar
2 eggs
1¾ cups self-rising flour
2 teaspoons baking powder

for the frosting
1½ cups confectioners' sugar
1 teaspoon butter
1 drop bergamot essential oil
   (optional)

1 Add the tea bags to the boiling water in a measuring jug, making sure they're all submerged. Cover with a plate and leave until cold.

2 Squeeze the tea bags to get as much liquid from them as possible, then discard the tea bags and measure out ⅔ cup of tea. Put this tea into a food processor or mixer (reserve the rest). Peel and mash the banana and add to the tea with the butter, brown sugar, eggs, flour, and baking powder, then whiz or beat until the mixture is light and fluffy.

3 Line a 7–8 inch cake pan with nonstick parchment paper, spoon the mixture in and gently level the surface. Bake in a preheated oven, 350°F, for 30–35 minutes, or until a toothpick inserted into the center comes out clean. Cool for a minute or so in the pan, then turn out onto a wire rack and leave until cold.

4 To make the frosting, put the confectioners' sugar into a saucepan with the butter, bergamot oil, if using, and 2 tablespoons of the remaining tea. Stir over the heat until the butter has melted. Pour over the top of the cake and allow to set.

The bergamot oil, which you can get at a healthfood store, intensifies the flavor of the Earl Grey in this stylish cake.

lemon and almond drizzle cake with berries

almonds sugar lemon

serves 4
preparation 25 minutes, plus
   standing
cooking 40–45 minutes

¾ cup butter, softened
¾ cup superfine sugar
2 eggs
finely grated zest of 1 lemon
1½ cups self-rising flour
½ cup ground almonds
1½ teaspoons baking powder
sour cream or crème fraîche,
   to serve

for the drizzle topping
4 tablespoons lemon juice
1¼ cups confectioners' sugar

for the berries
3 cups mixed berries, such as
   raspberries, strawberries,
   blueberries, or red currants,
   any stems and hulls removed
superfine sugar, to taste

1 Line a 1 lb 13 oz loaf pan with a strip of nonstick parchment paper to cover the base and narrow sides.

2 Beat together the butter, superfine sugar, eggs, and lemon zest until creamy, then stir in the flour, ground almonds, and baking powder.

3 Spoon the cake mixture into the prepared loaf pan and gently level the top. Bake in a preheated oven, 325°F, for 40–45 minutes, until risen and firm to a light touch and a toothpick inserted into the center comes out clean.

4 Five minutes before the cake is done, make the drizzle topping. Mix the lemon juice and confectioners' sugar in a small saucepan, then stir over a gentle heat until the confectioners' sugar has dissolved.

5 As soon as the cake comes out of the oven, prick the top all over and pour the confectioners' sugar mixture over the top. Set aside to cool, then remove the cake from the pan and strip off the paper.

6 Prepare the fruit an hour or so before you want to eat. Put it into a bowl, sprinkle over superfine sugar to taste and set aside for 1 hour, stirring from time to time. Taste and add a little more sugar if necessary. Serve the fruit and cake with a bowl of sour cream or crème fraîche.

fig tarte tatin with ginger cream

ginger figs pastry

serves 4
preparation 25 minutes
cooking 30 minutes

11 oz frozen ready-rolled all-butter
   puff pastry (see page 184)
3 tablespoons butter
1 lb 12 oz figs, halved
3 tablespoons superfine sugar
¼ cup toasted slivered almonds
   (optional)

for the ginger cream
generous cup heavy cream
3 pieces of preserved ginger,
   very finely chopped

1 Roll the pastry a little on a floured surface to make it a bit thinner if you can, then cut a circle to fit ½ inch larger than the top of an 8 inch tarte tatin pan or cake pan.

2 Melt the butter in the tarte tatin pan or in a skillet. Add the figs, cut-side down, and the sugar. Cook over a high heat for about 6 minutes, until the figs are slightly browned and caramelized.

3 If you're using a cake pan, put the figs, cut-side down, into it and scrape in all the gooey juice from the pan.

4 Put the pastry on top, tucking it down into the figs at the sides. Prick the pastry, then bake in a preheated oven, 400°F, for 20–25 minutes, until crisp and golden brown.

5 Meanwhile, make the ginger cream. Beat the cream until it is standing in soft peaks, then fold in the ginger. Transfer to a bowl and chill until required.

6 To serve, loosen the tarte with a knife, then invert over a plate. The figs will be on top. Scatter with toasted slivered almonds, if using, then leave to settle for a couple of minutes before serving with the ginger cream.

This is also delicious made with apricots. Make exactly as described, using 1 lb 12 oz apricots, halved and pitted, instead of the figs.

orange creams
with caramel and toffee sauce

sugar orange butter

serves 4
preparation 30 minutes,
  plus cooling
cooking 35 minutes

for the orange creams
1¼ cups heavy cream
2 pieces of pared orange zest
6 egg yolks
⅓ cup superfine sugar

for the oranges
4 ripe sweet juicy oranges
superfine sugar, to taste

for the toffee sauce
¼ cup butter
5 tablespoons heavy cream
4 tablespoons brown sugar

1 Line the base of 4 ramekins with disks of nonstick paper.

2 Put the cream and orange zest into a saucepan and bring to a boil. Remove from the heat and allow to cool slightly. Remove the orange zest.

3 Beat together the egg yolks and 2 tablespoons of the superfine sugar to blend, then gradually beat in the cream. Pour the mixture into the ramekins, stand them in a roasting pan and pour in boiling water to come half to three-quarters of the way up the sides of the ramekins. Bake in a preheated oven, 275°F, for about 30 minutes, or until the custards are just firm in the centers. Remove from the oven, cool, then chill.

4 Cut the skin and pith from the oranges, then cut the segments out of the white inner skin. Put the segments into a bowl with a little superfine sugar to taste if necessary and chill until required.

5 For the sauce, put the butter, cream, and brown sugar into a saucepan and heat gently for 2–3 minutes, to make a golden toffee sauce.

6 To serve, loosen the sides of the orange creams and turn one out onto each plate, then remove the lining paper. Top each with a thin layer of the remaining superfine sugar and heat with a cook's blowtorch to make a hard glazed golden topping. Alternatively, turn them out onto a heatproof plate that will fit under your broiler, top each with a thin layer of superfine sugar and broil them for 1–2 minutes to make the caramel, then carefully transfer each to a serving plate. Arrange some orange slices on each plate and drizzle some toffee sauce around the oranges. Serve at once.

This is a great mixture of flavors and textures. The orange creams can be topped with crisp shiny golden caramel if you have a cook's blowtorch, or you can place them under the broiler—either way, they're delectable.

individual pavlovas
with pomegranate and grenadine

cream grenadine eggs

serves 4
preparation 15 minutes,
  plus standing
cooking 40 minutes

2 egg whites
½ cup superfine sugar
1 teaspoon cornstarch
¼ teaspoon vinegar

for the filling
seeds from 2 ripe pomegranates
4 tablespoons grenadine
1¼ cups heavy cream, whipped

1 Put the egg whites into a large, clean bowl and beat until they are thick, glossy, and standing in peaks. Beat in the sugar 1 tablespoon at a time, then fold in the cornstarch and vinegar.

2 Spoon the meringue onto a large cookie sheet lined with nonstick paper, making 4 saucer-size circles, and hollow each out in the center a little. Bake in a preheated oven, 275°F, for about 40 minutes, or until crisp on the outside but still soft within. Cool on the cookie sheet.

3 While the pavlovas are cooking, put the pomegranate seeds into a small bowl with the grenadine and allow to steep.

4 To finish the pavlovas, spoon some whipped cream onto each, then top with the pomegranate seeds and their juice. Serve as soon as possible.

fruit sushi plate

vanilla lime fruit

(V)

serves 4
preparation 20 minutes,
    plus cooling
cooking 25 minutes

for the rice
¾ cup Japanese sushi rice
    or white "pudding" rice
¼ cup superfine sugar
13 oz can organic coconut milk
1 vanilla bean
juice of 1 lime

for the fruit
½ cup superfine sugar
½ cup water
1 lemon grass stalk, crushed
½ teaspoon dried red chili flakes
juice and pared zest of 1 lime
1 carambola, thinly sliced
1 large ripe papaya, peeled,
    seeded and sliced
2 kiwi fruits, peeled and sliced

1 Put the rice and sugar into a saucepan with the coconut milk and vanilla bean. Bring to a boil, then reduce the heat, cover the pan and allow to cook very gently for 20 minutes, or until the liquid has been absorbed and the rice is tender. Remove from the heat, gently stir in the lime juice and allow to cool.

2 Meanwhile, make an aromatic syrup for the fruit. Put the sugar and water in a saucepan with the lemon grass, chili flakes, and lime zest. Heat gently until the sugar has dissolved, then bring to a boil and remove from the heat.

3 Put the carambola in a single layer on a plate and pour the hot syrup over, together with the lemon grass and lime zest. Cover and leave until cold, then remove the lemon grass and lime zest, squeeze them to extract all the flavor and discard them. Sprinkle over the lime juice.

4 To serve, form the sweet sushi rice into small circles ¾ inch in diameter and ½ inch thick and arrange on plates. Top with carambola, papaya, and kiwi fruit slices and spoon the syrup over them. Serve the remaining fruit on the side.

A plate of sweet sushi rice and lemon grass-scented fruits makes a very pretty and refreshing dessert.

coconut and kaffir lime panna cotta

cream lime coconut

serves 4
preparation 15 minutes,
   plus steeping and setting
cooking 10 minutes

13 oz can organic coconut milk
⅔ cup heavy cream
3 kaffir lime leaves
grated zest of 1 lime
2 tablespoons superfine sugar
¼ oz package vegetarian gelatin
lime slices and fresh kaffir lime
   leaves (optional), to decorate

for the syrup
1 lemon grass stalk, crushed
juice and grated zest of 2 limes
6 tablespoons superfine sugar

1 Put the coconut milk and cream into a saucepan with the lime leaves and lime zest. Bring to a boil, then cover, remove from the heat and set aside until cold.

2 Remove and discard the lime leaves. Stir in the sugar, then sprinkle the gelatin over the top, stirring all the time to prevent lumps. Heat gently, stirring all the time, until the mixture just reaches boiling point, then remove from the heat.

3 Pour the mixture into 4 x ½ cup ramekins or molds and allow to set, but don't refrigerate.

4 To make the syrup, put the lemon grass, lime juice and zest, and the sugar into a saucepan and heat gently to dissolve the sugar. Remove from the heat and set aside until required. Remove the lemon grass before serving.

5 Turn the panna cotta out onto individual serving plates and drizzle each with a little syrup. Decorate with slices of lime and lime leaves, if desired.

nectarines roasted with lavender

butter fruit sugar

(V)

serves 4
preparation 10 minutes
cooking 25 minutes

3 tablespoons butter
3 tablespoons raw sugar
2–3 dried heads of lavender
6 nectarines, halved and pits
    removed
chilled Greek or whole milk yogurt,
    to serve

1 Select a shallow casserole dish that will hold all the nectarine halves in a single layer, grease generously with half the butter and sprinkle with half the sugar and half the lavender.

2 Place the nectarine halves, cut-side down, in the buttered casserole, dot with the rest of the butter and sprinkle with the remaining sugar and lavender.

3 Bake, uncovered, in a preheated oven, 350°F, for about 25 minutes, or until the nectarines are tender. Serve hot or warm, with some chilled Greek or whole milk yogurt.

The wonderful taste of summer on a plate—
and so easy to do.

strawberries in rose jello

berries juice sugar

(V)

serves 4
preparation 15 minutes,
  plus setting
cooking 5 minutes

4 tablespoons superfine sugar
1½ cups raspberry and
  cranberry juice
¼ oz package vegetarian gelatin
4 tablespoons rosewater
3 cups strawberries, hulled and
  sliced

1 Put the sugar into a saucepan with the raspberry and cranberry juice. Sprinkle the gelatin over the top, stirring all the time to avoid lumps. Heat gently, stirring, until the sugar has dissolved, then bring to a boil, boil for a few seconds and remove from the heat. Add the rosewater.

2 Blot the strawberries well on paper towels to dry them a bit, then divide between 4 glass dishes. Pour the gelatin mixture over the strawberries and allow to cool for an hour or so.

3 The mixture sets very quickly and needs to be eaten within a couple of hours, before the juice from the strawberries softens the gelatin too much. If this happens, it will still taste good. Don't put it into the refrigerator or it will become opaque.

sangria fruit salad with almond shortbreads

wine grapes brandy

serves 4
preparation 10 minutes,
   plus standing
cooking 15–20 minutes

juice and finely grated zest of
   1 orange
4 tablespoons superfine sugar
4 tablespoons red Spanish wine
1 tablespoon brandy
1 tablespoon Cointreau
2 oranges, skin and pith removed,
   cut into segments
1 apple, peeled and sliced
2 peaches, thinly sliced,
   pits removed
1 cup white grapes, halved and any
   seeds removed
sprigs of fresh mint

for the shortbreads
¾ cup butter
¼ cup superfine sugar
1½ cups all-purpose white flour
½ cup ground almonds
confectioners' sugar, to serve

1 Put the orange juice and zest into a large bowl with the superfine sugar, wine, brandy, and Cointreau. Add all the prepared fruit and some of the mint sprigs and stir gently, then set aside for at least 30 minutes in a cool place until required.

2 To make the shortbreads, beat together the butter and superfine sugar until light and fluffy, then stir in the flour and ground almonds to make a soft dough. Form this dough into 16 even-size ovals and place well apart on cookie sheets lined with nonstick paper. Press the cookies lightly with the prongs of a fork.

3 Bake in a preheated oven, 325°F, for 15 minutes, or until set and lightly browned. Cool on the cookie sheet, then dredge with confectioners' sugar. Serve with the fruit salad and decorate with the remaining sprigs of mint.

I associate sangria with holidays in the sun—and I wanted to turn those flavors into a dessert—hence this recipe.

pink champagne granita marbled with raspberries

berries fizz sugar

(V)

serves 4
preparation 15 minutes,
**   plus cooling and freezing**
cooking 5 minutes

1 cup water
1 cup, plus 2 tablespoons
   superfine sugar
1 bottle Pink Champagne
2¾ cups raspberries

1 Put the water into a saucepan with the 1 cup sugar. Heat gently until the sugar has dissolved, then bring to a boil and remove from the heat. Allow to cool.

2 Mix the cooled sugar syrup with the Champagne. Pour into a shallow container so that the mixture is about ½ inch deep and freeze, stirring the mixture from time to time as it becomes frozen around the edges. Because of the alcohol in the Champagne, it will take up to 4 hours to freeze, and will never become rock hard, so can be used straight from the freezer. It's fine to make it the day before needed.

3 To serve, first toss the raspberries in the remaining sugar and set aside for a few minutes until the sugar has dissolved. Put a few raspberries into 4 serving glasses. Give the granita a quick stir with a fork, then scrape some into the glasses, on top of the raspberries. Continue to layer the raspberries and granita into the glasses, then serve immediately.

4 You probably won't need all the granita—it might be called for as second helpings and it makes a wonderful pick-me-up for the cook (or anyone else!) the morning after, perhaps with some freshly squeezed pink grapefruit juice added. Incidentally, ordinary Champagne, rather than pink, is also great to use, but not as pretty.

This recipe makes the most wonderful ending to a special meal.

affogato with almond tuiles

coffee almonds cream

serves 4
preparation 30 minutes
cooking 15–20 minutes

2½ cups heavy or whipping cream
13 oz can skimmed condensed milk
⅔ cup strong espresso coffee

for the almond tuiles
1 egg white
¼ cup superfine sugar
¼ cup all-purpose white flour, sifted
2 tablespoons butter, melted
⅛ cup slivered almonds
flavorless vegetable oil such
   as grapeseed for greasing

1 To make the ice cream, whip the cream, with an electric beater for speed and ease, though you can do it by hand, until soft peaks form. Add the condensed milk to the cream and whip again until combined. Tip into a suitable container—a rigid plastic box is ideal—and freeze until firm.

2 To make the tuiles, beat the egg white until stiff, then beat in the sugar. Add the flour and butter alternately to make a smooth mixture. Place big teaspoons of the mixture well apart on a cookie sheet lined with nonstick paper (you'll probably get about 4 to a large sheet) and, using the back of the spoon, spread the mixture out to make rounds each about 4 inches in diameter. Sprinkle the top of each with slivered almonds, then bake for 4–5 minutes in a preheated oven, 350°F, until set and lightly browned, especially around the edges.

3 Remove from the oven and allow to cool for a minute or so until firm enough to lift from the cookie sheet. While this is happening, grease a rolling pin. Drape the tuiles over the rolling pin so that as they cool they become curved. Once they're cool they can be removed to a wire rack.

4 Continue with the rest of the mixture to make about 16 tuiles. When they're all cold, store in an airtight container until needed.

5 To serve, scoop the ice cream into 4 bowls. Pour a couple of tablespoons of the hot coffee over each and serve immediately, with the tuiles.

This is an easy-to-make yet wonderful ice cream. Although freshly brewed espresso is the perfect topping for this—whisper it quietly, instant espresso is also fine: by the time it has mixed with the ice cream, I defy anyone to tell the difference!

white chocolate gelato with citrus drizzle

orange milk lime

serves 4
preparation 15 minutes,
  plus cooling and freezing
cooking 15 minutes

3 cups milk
2 x 5 oz bars white chocolate,
  broken into pieces
1½ teaspoons cornstarch
½ cup heavy cream

for the citrus drizzle
juice and finely grated zest of
  1 orange
juice and finely grated rind of 1 lime
½ cup superfine sugar

1 To make the ice cream, put the milk into a saucepan and bring to a boil. Remove from the heat and stir in the chocolate.

2 Put the cornstarch in a small bowl with some of the cream and blend to a smooth paste. Reheat the chocolate milk, then tip it into the cornstarch mixture, stir and return it to the saucepan, along with the rest of the cream. Bring to a boil, stir for a minute or so until it thickens, then remove from the heat and allow to cool.

3 Pour the cooled mixture into a suitable container for freezing, put into the freezer and leave until solid, stirring from time to time during the freezing process if possible.

4 To make the citrus drizzle, put the orange and lime juices and zests into a small saucepan with the sugar and gently bring to a boil. Reduce the heat and simmer for about 5 minutes until reduced in quantity and slightly thickened (watch carefully as it burns easily). Set aside until required.

5 To serve, remove the ice cream from the freezer about 30 minutes in advance so that it can soften slightly, then scoop into bowls. Check the citrus drizzle: if it has become very thick, lighten it a bit by stirring in a teaspoon or so of hot water. Then swirl some citrus drizzle over the top of each portion and serve at once.

Because of its light consistency—
made mainly with milk rather than cream
—gelato takes longer to freeze than
normal ice cream and for this reason I
find it best to use the freezer rather than
an ice-cream maker. Having said that,
this gelato couldn't be simpler to make.

chocolate truffles

nuts chocolate cream

makes about 22
preparation 30 minutes,
   plus chilling
cooking 5 minutes

for the white chocolate and
   coffee truffles
4 oz white chocolate
2 tablespoons cold unsalted butter,
   cut into small pieces
⅓ cup cold heavy cream
½ teaspoon instant espresso coffee
1 teaspoon boiling water
4 oz melted white chocolate, sifted
   cocoa powder, or finely ground
   toasted hazelnuts, to coat

for the milk chocolate truffles
   with soft centers
4 oz milk chocolate
2 tablespoons cold unsalted butter,
   cut into small pieces
2 tablespoons cold heavy cream
1 teaspoon brandy (optional)
5 oz milk chocolate, sifted cocoa
   powder, or finely ground toasted
   hazelnuts, to coat

1 To make the white chocolate and coffee truffles, melt the white chocolate in a small bowl set over a pan of gently steaming water. Take the bowl off the heat and stir in first the butter and then the cream. Dissolve the coffee in the boiling water and stir into the mixture, then chill in the refrigerator until firm —about 1 hour.

2 Divide the white chocolate mixture into 10 even-size pieces and form into balls. Place these on nonstick paper and put into the freezer to chill thoroughly for about 1 hour.

3 To coat with chocolate, dip the frozen chocolates into the melted white chocolate—it will set very quickly—coating both sides. Alternatively, roll the truffles in cocoa powder or finely ground toasted hazelnuts. Put them on nonstick paper and chill in the refrigerator until required.

4 To make the milk chocolate truffles, melt the 4 oz milk chocolate in a small bowl as before, then remove from the heat and beat in the butter, cream, and brandy, if you're using this. Chill in the refrigerator until fairly firm, then proceed as described for the white truffles, using milk chocolate, cocoa powder, or nuts to coat.

5 Store all the truffles in the refrigerator until required.

These heavenly truffles have rich, creamy centers like Belgian chocolates and are absolutely worth the effort.

alfresco entertaining

I love eating outside: from the first day that's half warm enough to the last of an Indian summer, that's where I'll be … relishing the relaxed food that cries out to be eaten with the fingers, the strong flavors, the informality—and there's a good selection of it in this section.

plantain bhajis with fresh coconut chutney

chili lime cumin

(V)

serves 4 (makes about 20 bhajis)
preparation 20 minutes
cooking 15 minutes

1 cup besan
½–1 teaspoon dried red chili flakes
½ teaspoon turmeric
2 teaspoons coriander
2 teaspoons ground cumin
2 teaspoons cumin seeds
⅔–1 cup sparkling water
1 plantain, (about 11 oz)
canola or peanut oil for frying
salt, to taste

for the coconut chutney
3 oz fresh grated coconut
   (about ¼ of a coconut)
½ cup cilantro
juice and grated zest of 1 lime
1 teaspoon black mustard seeds

1 First make the chutney. Put the grated coconut, cilantro, and lime juice and zest into a food processor and whiz until combined. Stir in the mustard seeds and, if necessary, a little water to make a soft, creamy consistency. Set aside.

2 To make a batter, mix the besan, chili flakes, turmeric, coriander, ground and whole cumin seeds, and some salt with enough sparkling water to make a batter that will coat the back of the spoon.

3 When you are ready to serve the bhajis, heat 1 inch of oil in a skillet. Peel the plantain and cut it diagonally into slices about 1 inch thick.

4 Dip a slice of plantain into the batter, then put into the hot oil—it should sizzle immediately. Repeat with several more slices until the skillet is full. Turn the slices when the underside is golden brown and crisp. When they are done remove them with a slotted spoon onto crumpled paper towels. Serve at once in batches, with the chutney—or keep the first ones warm while you fry the rest, then serve all at once, hot and crisp.

zucchini and corn cakes
with chili sauce

garlic dill corn

(V)

serves 4
preparation 15 minutes
cooking 15 minutes

2 tablespoons olive oil, plus extra
   for pan-frying
8 oz baby corn, sliced into ¼ inch
   thick rounds
3 cups coarsely grated zucchini
   (about 12 oz)
3 garlic cloves, crushed
5 tablespoons masa harina
   (see page 184)
1 teaspoon ground cumin
1 teaspoon dried dill weed
salt and pepper, to taste
3 tablespoons chopped cilantro
red chili sauce, to serve

1 Heat the 2 tablespoons of olive oil in a large saucepan, then add the corn, zucchini and garlic. Cook gently, stirring often, for about 5 minutes until the vegetables are tender.

2 Add the masa harina, cumin, dill, and some salt and pepper and stir well over the heat for 2–3 minutes, until the mixture is very thick and holds together well. Set aside until cool enough to handle, then form into 2 inch diameter cakes. You should make about 12–14.

3 Heat a little olive oil in a skillet and fry the cakes on both sides until golden brown and crisp. Drain on paper towels, then serve with red chili sauce for dipping.

As these little corncakes hold together so well, you could also cook them on a barbecue instead of frying them.

chickpea and lemon cakes

tahini lemon garlic

serves 4
preparation 20 minutes
cooking 15 minutes

2 x 14 oz cans chickpeas
2 garlic cloves, crushed
4 tablespoons freshly squeezed
   lemon juice
2 tablespoons tahini
salt and pepper, to taste
lemon slices, to garnish

for the coating
6 tablespoons cornstarch
5 tablespoons water
¼ cup dried bread crumbs
canola or peanut oil for deep-frying

1 Strain the chickpeas well, reserving the liquid. Put them into a food processor with the garlic, lemon juice, tahini, and some salt and pepper and whiz until smooth. If the mixture is fairly stiff, add a little of the reserved chickpea liquid and whiz again. The texture needs to be light and fluffy, but firm enough to be formed into "cakes."

2 Put the cornstarch into a bowl and mix in the water to make a thick coating paste. Form the chickpea mixture into balls, dip each into the cornstarch paste and then into the dried bread crumbs, turning them to make sure they're thoroughly coated.

3 Heat sufficient oil in a pan for deep-frying to 350–375°F, or until a cube of bread browns in 30 seconds, and fry the cakes for 2–3 minutes. Drain on paper towels and serve at once, garnished with lemon slices.

These savory cakes have all the flavor
and creamy texture of hummus within a
crisp outer coating.

adzuki, rice, and ginger balls with teriyaki dip

beans plums ginger

(V)

makes 18
preparation 20 minutes
cooking 1 hour 5 minutes

⅓ cup adzuki beans
½ cup brown rice
2 teaspoons grated fresh ginger root
1¼ cups water
2 teaspoons lemon juice
flesh from 2–3 umeboshi plums or
    1–2 teaspoons umeboshi paste
    (see page 185)
2–3 tablespoons sesame seeds
salt and pepper, to taste

for the dip
3 tablespoons shoyu or tamari
3 tablespoons mirin

1 Cover the beans with water and bring to a boil, then reduce the heat, half cover the pan and simmer for 45 minutes, or until tender. Drain.

2 Put the rice and ginger into a saucepan with the measured water. Bring to a boil, then reduce the heat, cover the pan and allow to cook over a very gentle heat for 30–40 minutes, or until the rice is tender and all the water has been absorbed.

3 Put the rice into a food processor with the beans, lemon juice, umeboshi, and some salt and pepper and whiz to a thick mixture that holds together.

4 Put the sesame seeds onto a large plate, then break off large marble-size pieces of the rice mixture and roll them in the seeds to form 18 balls. Place the rice balls on a baking sheet and bake in a preheated oven, 350°F, for 20 minutes, or until crisp on the outside.

5 To make the dip, mix the shoyu or tamari with the mirin in a small bowl and serve with the rice balls.

eggplant steaks with mint glaze

lime honey mint

V

serves 4
preparation 10 minutes,
   plus marinating
cooking 20 minutes

2 large eggplants, stems trimmed
juice of 1 lime
2 tablespoons toasted sesame oil
2 tablespoons honey or
   maple syrup
4 tablespoons chopped mint

1 Cut each eggplant lengthwise into 4 thick slices. Cut cross-hatching on both surfaces of the slices—on two of them you will be cutting the skin. Place the eggplant slices on a shallow tray or broiler pan.

2 Mix the lime juice with the sesame oil and honey or maple syrup. Drizzle this over the surfaces of the eggplant, turning them over to drench both sides. Allow to marinate for 30 minutes, or up to 8 hours.

3 Broil the eggplant slices under a hot broiler or grill over a barbecue until browned on one side, then turn over to grill the other side until both sides are tender and lightly browned—about 20 minutes.

4 Sprinkle with the chopped mint and serve at once.

So simple—and so delicious—this has become one of my favorite ways to cook eggplant.

spice-crusted tofu with maple glaze

V

serves 4
preparation 10 minutes
cooking 10 minutes

3 tablespoons paprika
3 teaspoons ground cumin
3 teaspoons coriander
1½ teaspoons salt
3 x 8 oz blocks firm tofu, drained
6 tablespoons olive oil
9 tablespoons boiling water
6 tablespoons freshly squeezed
    lemon juice
4½ tablespoons maple syrup
½ cup pine nuts, toasted
pepper, to taste

1 Mix the paprika with the ground cumin and coriander, the salt, and a grinding of black pepper and spread out on a plate.

2 Cut the tofu blocks in half, then slice each half horizontally to make 4 "steaks." Dip the tofu in the spices, coating all sides.

3 Heat the olive oil in a skillet, add the tofu and cook until brown and crusty on one side, 4–5 minutes, then turn the pieces over and cook the other side.

4 While the tofu is cooking, mix the boiling water with the lemon juice and maple syrup. Add this mixture to the pan—it will bubble up and disappear very quickly, leaving a sticky glaze.

5 Transfer the tofu to a serving dish, sprinkle with the pine nuts and serve immediately.

chunky smoked cheese and parsley sausages

shallots parsley

makes 12
preparation 10 minutes
cooking 5–10 minutes

2 x 5 oz packages Bavarian
   smoked cheese, grated
3 cups soft wholewheat
   bread crumbs
6 tablespoons chopped parsley
2 shallots
olive oil for pan-frying or brushing
salt and pepper, to taste
hot pepper sauce, to serve

1 Put the grated cheese, bread crumbs, parsley, shallots, and a little salt and pepper into a food processor and whiz to a smooth mixture that holds together. Form into 12 fat chunky sausages.

2 Pan-fry the sausages in a little hot olive oil for 5 minutes, or brush all over with olive oil and cook on a barbecue, turning them so that they become crisp and golden brown all over.

3 Serve at once with hot pepper sauce, while they are hot and crisp on the outside, melting and tender within.

dough ball, halloumi, and olive skewers

butter cheese lemons

serves 4
preparation 20 minutes,
   plus rising
cooking 10–15 minutes

2 x 8 oz blocks halloumi cheese,
   drained
24 large green olives, pitted
olive oil for brushing

for the dough balls
2 cups white bread flour
½ package active dry yeast
1 teaspoon salt
¾ cup warm water
2 tablespoons olive oil

for the lemon butter
juice and grated zest of ½ lemon
½ cup soft butter

1 To make the dough balls, put the flour into a food processor fitted with a plastic dough blade. Add the yeast, salt, water, and olive oil and pulse until a dough forms, then blend for 1 minute. Leave, with the lid on, for 45 minutes, or until the dough has doubled in size.

2 Divide the dough into 24 equal pieces and roll into marble-size balls.

3 Cut each block of halloumi into 12 cubes. Thread a dough ball onto a skewer followed by an olive and a cube of halloumi; repeat twice so that each skewer contains 3 dough balls, pieces of cheese, and olives. Brush lightly with olive oil and place on a broiler pan or baking sheet. When all the skewers are done, cover them with a piece of plastic or a clean damp cloth and leave for 50–60 minutes for the dough balls to rise.

4 These skewers can be cooked in the oven, at 400°F, under the broiler, or on a barbecue: preheat these in advance, then cook the skewers, turning them when the first side is done. They will take about 5 minutes on each side.

5 To make the lemon butter, beat the lemon juice and zest into the softened butter and serve with the dough ball skewers.

The dough balls are quick and easy to make, but, if you prefer, use store-bought frozen dough balls, thawed. You need 8 skewers for this recipe—if you use wooden ones soak them in cold water for 10 minutes before use to prevent them burning.

mexican tart with cumin pastry

eggs peppers chili

serves 4
preparation 30 minutes
cooking 1 hour

2 onions, chopped
2 green bell peppers, cored, seeded
  and chopped
1 tablespoon olive oil
2 x 13 oz cans chopped tomatoes
½ teaspoon dried red pepper flakes
5 very fresh eggs
salt and pepper, to taste

for the cumin pastry
2 cups all-purpose flour
2 teaspoons cumin seeds
½ cup butter
about 4 tablespoons cold water

1 To make the cumin pastry, put the flour and cumin seeds into a bowl, add the butter and blend with your fingertips until the mixture resembles fine bread crumbs. Add enough cold water—3–4 tablespoons—to mix to a malleable dough. Turn the dough out onto a lightly floured surface and knead briefly. Roll out to fit a deep greased 12 inch tart pan, ease the pastry into place, then press down and trim the edges. Prick the base, then cover it with nonstick paper and some dried beans to weigh the pastry down.

2 Bake the tart shell in a preheated oven, 400°F, for 20 minutes, until set and crisp. Remove the paper and beans and bake the tart shell for an additional 10 minutes until the base is crisp. Remove the shell from the oven and reduce the oven temperature to 350°F.

3 Meanwhile, make the filling. Fry the onions and green peppers in the olive oil, covered, for 5 minutes, until beginning to get tender, then add the tomatoes and pepper flakes and simmer, uncovered, over a moderate heat for 25–30 minutes, or until very thick, stirring from time to time to prevent sticking. Remove from the heat and season with salt and pepper.

4 Spoon the tomato filling evenly into the tart shell. Make a depression in the center, for one of the eggs, and four more evenly spaced around the edge. Break the eggs into the depressions and season lightly.

5 Cover the tart with foil, return to the oven and bake for about 20 minutes, or until the eggs are set.

This dramatic-looking tart has a hot and spicy red filling topped with eggs. To help the eggs set neatly, use very fresh eggs taken straight from the refrigerator.

potato and white truffle torte

butter garlic parsley

serves 4
preparation 20 minutes
cooking 30 minutes

2 lb potatoes, peeled and
    cut into ¼ inch thick slices
2 garlic cloves, crushed
3 tablespoons butter
2 oz white truffle, wiped, or 3¼ oz jar
    porcini mushrooms in a
    vegetarian white truffle paste
    (see page 184)
2½ cups grated Parmesan-style
    cheese
salt and pepper, to taste
flat leaf parsley, to garnish

1 Cook the potatoes in boiling water to cover for about 10 minutes, or until tender but not soft. Drain.

2 Mix the garlic into the butter and use half to grease generously a 9–10 inch springform pan. Arrange a layer of potato in the pan, then grate some of the truffle over the top, or spread some truffle paste over the potatoes. Sprinkle with cheese and season with salt and pepper.

3 Continue these layers, seasoning with salt and pepper between each layer, until you have used all the ingredients, ending with a layer of potato and one of cheese. Dot with the remaining butter.

4 Bake in a preheated oven, 450°F, for about 20 minutes, or until golden brown and crisp on top.

5 Remove the sides of the pan, slide the torte (on its base) onto a warmed plate, snip some parsley over the top and serve at once.

This has a wonderful rich and seductive flavor. White truffle is fantastic in this if available, but you can also make a very good version using Porcini and White Truffle Paste. It's very rich: great with a refreshing green salad.

cavalo nero and goat cheese torte

raisins nuts cheese

serves 4
preparation 20 minutes
cooking 25 minutes

14 oz bunch of cavalo nero,
   (black leaf kale) tough stems
   removed, leaves shredded
2 x 3½ oz packages soft goat
   cheese, cut into rough chunks
¼ cup raisins
12 oz frozen ready-rolled all-butter
   puff pastry (see page 184)
¼ cup pine nuts
1 oz Pecorino, or other hard Italian
   Parmesan-style cheese, grated
salt and pepper, to taste

1 Cook the cavalo nero in 1 inch of boiling water for 7–10 minutes, or until tender. Drain very well and allow to cool.

2 Add the goat cheese and raisins to the cavalo nero, along with some salt and pepper, and mix gently but thoroughly.

3 Roll the pastry a little more, then cut out a circle about 13 inches in diameter. Lay the pastry circle on a baking sheet.

4 Spoon the cavolo nero mixture onto the pastry circle, leaving about 1 inch clear all around the edges and smoothing it level. Then fold up the edges and press them together to make a crust. Sprinkle the top with pine nuts and grated cheese. Cut some long strips from the remaining pastry and make a lattice over the top of the filling.

5 Bake the torte in a preheated oven, 400°F, for about 15 minutes, or until it is puffed up and golden brown on top. Eat the torte hot, warm, or cold.

mimosa egg salad with tarragon

eggs lettuce mayo

serves 4
preparation 10 minutes
cooking 10 minutes

8 eggs, hard-cooked
4 tablespoons mayonnaise
½ cup chopped fresh tarragon
8 crisp, cup-shaped lettuce leaves
  from an ordinary butter head or
  iceberg lettuce
salt and pepper, to taste

1 Separate the egg whites from the yolks and chop both finely.

2 Mix the egg whites and all but 1 tablespoon of the yolks with the mayonnaise and most of the chopped tarragon. Season with salt and pepper.

3 Arrange the lettuce leaves in a single layer in a shallow serving dish. Spoon the egg mixture loosely into each lettuce leaf—it doesn't have to be too neat and tidy—then scatter the remaining chopped egg yolk and tarragon over the top and serve.

Very pretty and refreshing, this is great as an accompaniment or, on individual plates, as an appetizer.

jamaican jerk sweet potato

spices lime chives

serves 4
preparation 20 minutes
cooking 20 minutes

4 sweet potatoes, about 12 oz each
lime wedges, to serve (optional)

for the jerk spice paste
1 onion, roughly chopped
1 red chili, seeded
4 garlic cloves
4 teaspoons dried thyme
2 teaspoons allspice
1 teaspoon ground cinnamon
½ teaspoon ground nutmeg
2 tablespoons olive oil
1 teaspoon salt
1 teaspoon pepper

for the chive yogurt
2 tablespoons chopped chives
2¼ cups plain yogurt
salt and pepper, to taste

1 To make the jerk paste, put all the ingredients into a food processor and whiz to a paste.

2 Cut the sweet potatoes into wedges about ¼ inch thick—they need to be thin enough to cook through without burning. Spread the cut surfaces of the wedges with the jerk paste and place under a hot broiler or on a barbecue grid. Cook for 5 minutes on each side, or until the sweet potato is tender to the point of a knife and the jerk paste is crunchy and slightly charred.

3 Stir the chives into the yogurt along with some salt and pepper and put into a small bowl.

4 Serve the sweet potato wedges at once while still sizzling hot, accompanied by the chive yogurt, wedges of lime, and plenty of soft bread, if desired.

It's easy to make your own jerk paste, but for a very fast option, use a store-bought one instead.

leek rice with almonds and red pepper mayo

rice olives peppers

(V)

serves 4
preparation 20 minutes
cooking 20–25 minutes

1¼ cups white basmati rice
1 teaspoon turmeric
2 cups water
1 lb leeks, cut into 1 inch pieces
2 tablespoons freshly squeezed
    lemon juice
1 tablespoon olive oil
2 teaspoons black mustard seeds
4 tablespoons toasted slivered
    almonds
⅓ cup small green olives
salt and pepper, to taste

for the red pepper mayo
1 large red bell pepper, halved,
    cored, and seeded
2 tablespoons red wine vinegar
6 tablespoons olive oil
2 teaspoons superfine sugar

1 Put the rice into a saucepan with the turmeric and water. Bring to a boil, then turn the heat down as low as possible, cover the pan and allow to cook for about 10 minutes. Remove from the heat without removing the lid and allow to stand for 5–10 minutes.

2 Meanwhile, cook the leeks in boiling water to cover for about 10 minutes, or until tender. Drain.

3 Add the lemon juice to the rice along with some salt and pepper, stirring gently, then mix the leeks into the rice.

4 Heat the olive oil in a small pan, add the mustard seeds and fry for 1–2 minutes, or until they're sizzling. Add to the leek mixture, along with the slivered almonds and olives.

5 To make the mayo, put the red pepper halves cut-side down on a broiler pan and cook under a hot broiler for about 10 minutes, or until black and blistered in places. Cool, then strip off the skin. Blend the peppers with the wine vinegar, olive oil, sugar, and some salt and pepper in a food processor, blender, or using an immersion blender, to make a smooth, thick, brick-red sauce. Serve with the rice. This dish can be served hot, warm, or cold.

buckwheat and mango tabbouleh

mango mint lime

V

serves 4
preparation 10 minutes,
  plus standing
cooking 3–4 minutes

1⅓ cups raw buckwheat
1 large ripe juicy mango
bunch of mint, chopped
juice of 1 lime
salt and pepper, to taste

1 Put the buckwheat into a dry saucepan and stir over a moderate heat for 3–4 minutes, or until the buckwheat smells toasty and is turning light golden brown. Remove from the heat, cover with boiling water and set aside for 10–15 minutes to soften.

2 Cut the mango down each side of the seed. Remove all the skin, slice the flesh and put into a bowl.

3 When the buckwheat has softened—when you can squash a grain between your finger and thumb—drain it and put into a bowl. Stir in the mango, mint, lime juice, and some salt and pepper. Eat at once or store in a cool place for a few hours.

You can buy buckwheat at organic and healthfood stores. Be sure to get the raw, untoasted type.

green olives with mixed peppercorns and coriander

oil garlic olives

(V)

serves 4
preparation 10 minutes,
** plus marinating**

11½ oz can green queen olives in
  brine, drained
2 garlic cloves, finely sliced
1 lemon
1 tablespoon coriander seeds
1 tablespoon mixed peppercorns—
  black, white, green, pinks and
  pimiento
extra virgin olive oil for marinating

1 Put the olives into a bowl with the garlic. Cut thin strips of zest from half the lemon, using a zester if possible, and add to the olives. Slice the remaining half of the lemon thinly, then cut the slices into smaller pieces again and add to the bowl.

2 Crush the coriander seeds and peppercorns coarsely using a mortar and pestle or by putting them into a strong plastic bag and bashing with a rolling pin. Add to the bowl, then pour in enough olive oil to cover the olives and allow to marinate for at least 1 hour, or longer if there's time.

Why marinate your own olives when you can buy them? Because they're so easy to make yourself and you can rustle them up when you want them from pantry ingredients—but most of all, because these are divine!

lima bean salad with sweet chili dressing

beans celery onion

(V)

serves 4
preparation 5 minutes

2 x 14 oz cans lima beans,
   drained and rinsed
1 teaspoon dried crushed
   red pepper
2 teaspoons maple syrup
2 tablespoons rice vinegar
2 teaspoons toasted sesame oil
2 teaspoons shoyu or tamari
2 scallions, thinly sliced
3 4 tablespoons roughly chopped
   celery leaves
½ cup salted peanuts, crushed
pepper, to taste

1 Put the lima beans into a bowl, add the crushed red pepper, maple syrup, rice vinegar, sesame oil, shoyu or tamari, and a grinding of pepper and stir gently to mix.

2 Add the scallions and celery leaves, then stir again. Add the crushed peanuts just before serving, so that they remain crisp.

quick yeasted herb and garlic flat bread

thyme salt yeast

serves 4
preparation 20 minutes,
   plus rising
cooking 20–30 minutes

4 cups white bread flour
1 package active dry yeast
2 teaspoons sea salt plus extra
   for sprinkling
1½ cups warm water
6 tablespoons olive oil
4 tablespoons chopped thyme

1 Put the flour into a food processor fitted with a plastic dough blade. Add the yeast, the 2 teaspoons of salt, the water, and 2 tablespoons of the olive oil and pulse until a dough forms, then blend for 1 minute. Leave, with the lid on, for 45 minutes, or until the dough has doubled in size.

2 Add the chopped thyme and process briefly to mix, then remove the dough from the machine, divide in half and press each into a wide 1 lb 13 oz loaf pan or 8 inch square pan. Cover with plastic wrap and leave for 1 hour to rise.

3 Press your fingers into the top of the bread a few times and drizzle the rest of the olive oil over the loaves and into the holes, then sprinkle with some sea salt.

4 Bake the loaves in a preheated oven, 400°F, for 20–30 minutes, or until the loaves are golden brown on top and sound hollow when turned out of the pans and tapped on the base. (The timing will depend on the exact size of your pan—the deeper the dough in the tin, the longer it will take to cook.)

5 Cool on a wire rack, or wrap each loaf in a clean dishtowel and allow to cool slowly if you want the bread to have a soft crust.

This is a very easy bread that you both mix and let rise in the food processor! It couldn't be simpler.

honey corn muffins

seeds eggs honey

makes 12
preparation 20 minutes
cooking 10–15 minutes

¾ cup wholewheat flour
⅔ cup coarse cornmeal
2½ teaspoons baking powder
3 tablespoons sunflower seeds
2 eggs
¾ cup milk
6 tablespoons honey
2 tablespoons olive oil

1 Line a muffin pan with 12 paper bake cups.

2 Put the flour into a bowl with the cornmeal, the baking powder, and half the sunflower seeds.

3 Beat together the eggs, milk, honey, and olive oil, then stir quickly into the dry ingredients—don't mix it too much.

4 Divide the mixture between the paper cups and sprinkle the remaining sunflower seeds on top of each muffin. Bake in a preheated oven, 400°F, for 10–15 minutes until risen, golden, and firm to a light touch. These muffins are delicious for breakfast straight from the oven, or can be reheated for a few minutes before serving.

fruit fajita pudding

pears coconut grapes

serves 4
preparation 25 minutes
cooking 15 minutes

for the fajitas
1 cup all-purpose white flour
2 teaspoons superfine sugar
2 eggs
1¼ cups milk and water mixed
a little flavorless oil, such as
    groundnut, for pan-frying

for the fruit salad
2 ripe pears, peeled and cut into
    bite-size pieces
⅔ cup small strawberries, hulled
¾ cup purple or red seedless
    grapes, halved
2 ripe kiwi fruit, peeled and sliced
juice of 1 orange

to serve
toasted almonds or coconut
whipped heavy cream
maple syrup
superfine sugar
slices of lime

1 All the preparation for this can be done in advance. First make the fajitas, which are in fact sweet pancakes. Put the flour, sugar, eggs, and most of the milk and water into a blender or food processor and blend to a smooth batter, adding the rest of the liquid if necessary to make a consistency like light cream. Alternatively, sift the flour into a bowl, add the sugar and break in the eggs. Beat together, adding the liquid gradually to make a smooth batter.

2 Heat 1 tablespoon of oil in a skillet. When it's hot, swirl the oil around the pan and tip any excess into a cup. Pour in a good 2 tablespoons of the batter and tip the pan so that it spreads all over the base—you may need a bit more or less batter, depending on the size of your skillet, but the pancakes need to be thick enough to be rolled around the fruit salad filling later—more robust than delicate crêpes!

3 After a minute or so, when the top of the pancake has set, flip it over with a spatula to cook the other side, which will take only a few seconds. Put the pancake onto a plate and continue to make more in the same way, piling them up on the plate. Grease the skillet with more oil as required.

4 Make the fruit salad by mixing all the fruits together and adding the orange juice. Put into a serving bowl and keep cool.

5 Serve a pile of fajitas with the bowl of fruit salad and small bowls of toasted almonds or coconut, whipped heavy cream, maple syrup, superfine sugar and lime slices, for people to help themselves. Plenty of napkins and finger bowls might be a good idea.

This sweet version of fajitas makes a fun help-yourself pudding, ideal for an informal meal with friends.

party time

Party time is show-off time—and here are

some stunning recipes. Some are tiny—

"just a mouthful"—but none are difficult.

Some can be served cold, others made

and reheated or cooked at the last minute.

Serve 3–4 different types; each type on its

own platter; and allow 5–7 nibbles per person.

canapés: bruschette with three toppings

tahini garlic oil

makes 24
preparation 40 minutes
cooking 30 minutes

1 rosemary loaf, or 1 baguette
   and dried rosemary
olive oil
salt and pepper, to taste

for the eggplant caviar

2 eggplants
1–2 garlic cloves, crushed
2 tablespoons tahini
2 tablespoons olive oil plus extra
   to garnish
2 tablespoons freshly squeezed
   lemon juice
garlic sprouts, to garnish (optional)

for the goat cheese with
red onion and beet

2 cups thinly sliced red onions
1 tablespoon olive oil
1 tablespoon superfine sugar
1 tablespoon red wine vinegar
2 cups diced cooked beet
8 oz soft goat cheese
rosemary leaves, to garnish

for the chestnut pâté

7 oz vacuum pack whole
   peeled chestnuts
1 tablespoon butter
1 garlic clove, crushed
2 tablespoons freshly squeezed
   lemon juice
paprika pepper (or finely chopped
   small sweet red peppers from a
   jar) and sprigs of thyme, to garnish

1 Start by making the bruschette. Slice the bread, then brush each slice on both sides with olive oil. If you're using a plain baguette, sprinkle each piece on both sides with a good pinch of crushed rosemary. Place the bread on a baking sheet and bake in a preheated oven, 300°F, for about 20 minutes until crisp. Cool on wire racks. They can be made up to 1 week in advance and kept in an airtight container.

2 Next make the fillings. For the eggplant caviar, prick the eggplants in several places, then cook them under a very hot broiler for 25–30 minutes until soft and well charred. Cool slightly, then peel off the skin and whiz the eggplant to a pale cream with the garlic, tahini, the 2 tablespoons of olive oil, and the lemon juice. Season with salt and pepper and chill until required.

3 For the caramelized onion and beet, cook the onions in the olive oil in a large saucepan, covered, for about 15 minutes until they're very tender, stirring them every 5 minutes. Add the sugar, wine vinegar, and beet, then simmer gently, uncovered, for 10–15 minutes. Remove from the heat, season, and cool.

4 For the chestnut pâté, put the chestnuts into a food processor with the butter, garlic, and lemon juice. Whiz to a fairly smooth puree and season with salt and pepper.

5 To prepare the bruschette, spread one-third of the bases with eggplant caviar and garnish with a drizzle of olive oil and a few garlic sprouts, if desired. Spread another third of the bases with goat cheese, top with caramelized onion and beet and a piece of rosemary. Spread the remaining bruschette with chestnut pâté and garnish with a dusting of paprika pepper or sweet red peppers and thyme sprigs.

mini carrot and cardamom tarte tatins

carrots oil pastry

makes 16
preparation 25 minutes
cooking 35 minutes

1½ lb carrots, very thinly sliced
1 large garlic clove, crushed
3 tablespoons olive oil
¾ cup water
1½ teaspoons superfine sugar
20 cardamom pods
12 oz frozen ready-rolled all-butter
    puff pastry (see page 184)
salt and pepper, to taste

1 Put the carrots into a saucepan with the garlic, olive oil, water, sugar, and some salt and pepper.

2 Crush the cardamom and discard the pods. Crush the seeds a little, then add to the saucepan. Bring to a boil, then reduce the heat, cover the pan and cook gently for about 10 minutes, or until the carrots are tender and glossy, and the water has disappeared. If there is still water left, remove the lid of the pan and boil the liquid rapidly until it has disappeared. Cool.

3 Line an 8½ x 12½ inch jelly roll pan with nonstick paper. Spread the carrots evenly over the bottom and cover with the pastry, pressing it down and trimming it to fit. Prick the pastry all over, then bake in a preheated oven, 400°F, for 15 minutes until puffy, golden brown, and crisp.

4 Allow the tart to cool completely, then turn it out onto a board so that the carrot is on top. Using a sharp round cutter, 1½ inches in diameter, carefully cut out 16 circles. You may need to use a sharp knife in addition to the cutter to get through the pastry.

5 Just before serving, put the little tarte tatins onto an ovenproof serving dish and pop them into the oven for a few minutes to warm through.

With their crisp flaky pastry bases and glossy orange tops of tender, melting carrot, these are gorgeous and not difficult to make.

mini watercress roulade slices

watercress eggs cheese

makes 18
preparation 25 minutes
cooking 12–15 minutes

2 tablespoons butter
3 cups finely chopped watercress
3 eggs
⅓ cup garlic and herb cream cheese
salt and pepper, to taste

1 Melt the butter in a saucepan, add the watercress and cook over a moderate heat for about 3 minutes, or until the watercress has wilted.

2 Puree the watercress in a food processor, then add the eggs and some salt and pepper and whiz until combined.

3 Line an 8½ x 12½ inch jelly roll pan with a piece of nonstick paper and pour the mixture in, making sure it flows into the corners. Bake in a preheated oven, 400°F, for about 12 minutes, or until set. Remove from the oven and allow to cool.

4 Turn the roulade out onto a piece of nonstick paper and strip off the backing paper.

5 Beat the cream cheese in a bowl until soft, adding 1–2 tablespoons of hot water if necessary, then spread evenly over the top of the roulade.

6 With the long side facing you, make an incision about ¼ inch in from the edge, but don't cut right through. Bend this piece of roulade up, pressing it against the filling, then continue to roll it firmly to make a small jelly roll. Wrap in nonstick paper until required, then unwrap and cut into 18 little slices to serve.

These are really very easy to do, and look and taste impressive.

asian omelet wraps

radish mirin sesame

makes 20
preparation 30 minutes
cooking 15 minutes

4 inch piece of cucumber, peeled
4 scallions
1 tablespoon rice vinegar
1 tablespoon shoyu or tamari
1 tablespoon mirin
4 eggs
toasted sesame oil
salt and pepper, to taste

to garnish
sesame seeds
radish roses
scallion tassels

1 Cut the cucumber and scallions into matchsticks about 2 inches long. Put them into a shallow dish and add the rice vinegar, shoyu or tamari, and the mirin, then mix gently and set aside.

2 Beat the eggs with some salt and pepper. Coat a skillet thinly with sesame oil and heat.

3 Pour about 1 tablespoon of the beaten egg into the skillet. Let it run a little, but tilt the skillet so that the omelet stays as round as possible. When the top has set completely, lift the omelette from the pan with a spatula, roll it up lightly, put it on a plate and continue making another 19 omelets in the same way, until all the egg has been used.

4 Unroll one of the omelets, put a few matchsticks of cucumber and one of scallion in the center and re-roll it. Place on a serving dish, seam-side down. Make the rest in the same way, arranging them all around the edge of a plate, like the spokes of a wheel.

5 Sprinkle with a few sesame seeds and put some radish roses and scallion tassels in the center of the plate to garnish. Keep cool until required.

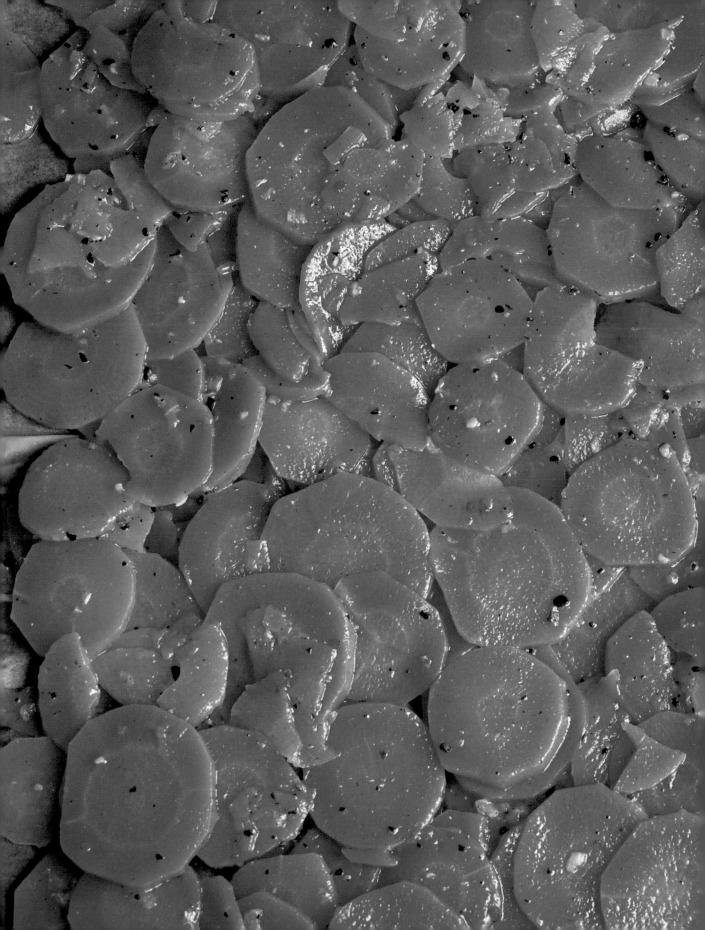

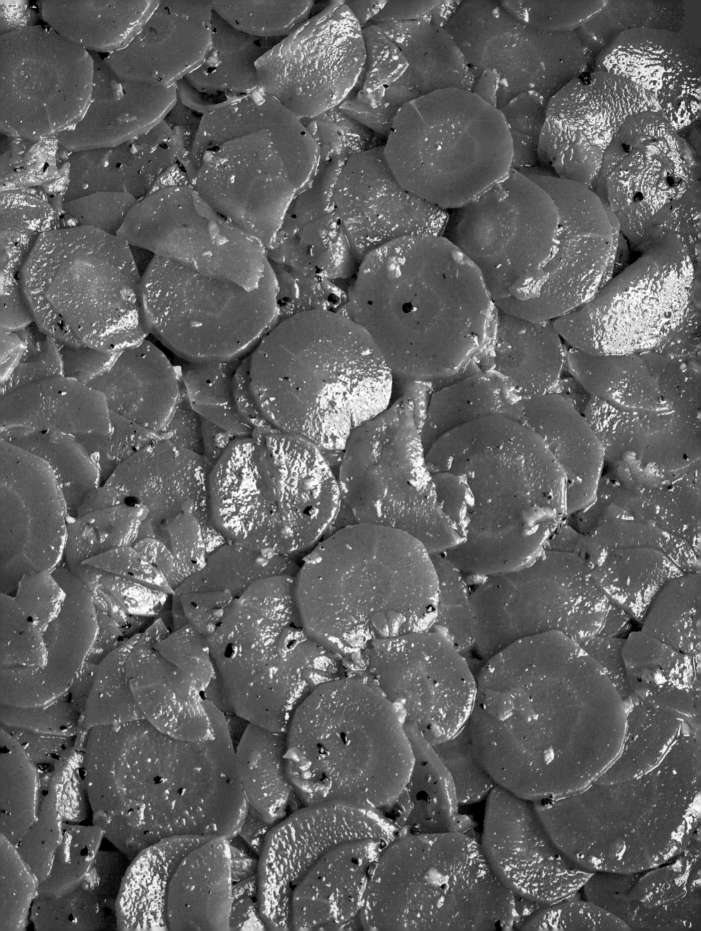

tiny tortillas

chives cheese cream

makes 20
preparation 15 minutes
cooking 30 minutes

1 lb potatoes, peeled and cut into
   even-size pieces
4 scallions, chopped
1 red bell pepper, cored, seeded,
   and very finely chopped
2 eggs, beaten
olive oil for frying
½ cup grated Gruyère cheese
5–6 cherry tomatoes, sliced
salt and pepper, to taste
⅔ cup sour cream and
   2 tablespoons chopped chives,
   to garnish (optional)

1 Cover the potatoes in boiling water and cook for about 10 minutes until they are just tender. Drain and cool.

2 Cut the potatoes into small cubes—about 1 inch—then mix with the scallions, red pepper, eggs, and some salt and pepper.

3 Heat a little olive oil in a skillet. Put heaping dessertspoons of the tortilla mixture into the hot oil, forming them into circles, and cook gently for about 5 minutes, or until the bases of the tortillas are golden brown and the tops have more or less set. Remove from the skillet onto a plate lined with paper towels and keep cool until you want to serve them.

4 Place the tortillas, in a single layer, on a flat ovenproof plate. Top each tortilla with a little Gruyère and a slice of tomato, then pop them under a hot broiler or into a hot oven for about 5 minutes, or until they are heated through and the tops are golden brown. Garnish each with a teaspoon of sour cream and some chopped chives, if desired, and serve at once.

These are delectable as they are, garnished with a spoonful of chive sour cream, or served with a bowl of sour cream and chives for dipping.

mini feta and sun-dried tomato muffins

basil feta tomato

makes 30
preparation 10 minutes
cooking 10 minutes

2 tablespoons olive oil plus extra
    for greasing
1 egg
2 tablespoons sun-dried tomato
    paste
2 tablespoons water
1 cup all-purpose white flour
2 teaspoons baking powder
8 oz feta cheese, cut into tiny dice
8 sun-dried tomatoes in oil,
    drained and finely chopped
4 tablespoons lightly chopped basil
salt and pepper, to taste

1 Line the bases of a 12-hole mini-muffin pan, each hole measuring ¾ inch across and about 1.5 cm (¾ inch) deep, with circles of nonstick paper, then brush them with olive oil. Or line them with mini paper bake cups if you have them.

2 Beat together the rest of the olive oil, the egg, tomato paste, and water.

3 Sift together the flour and baking powder into a bowl, then mix in the feta, sun-dried tomatoes, basil, and some salt and pepper. Make a well in the center and add the egg mixture. Stir until just combined—do not over mix.

4 Spoon into the mini-muffin pan holes or cups, filling them well, and bake in a preheated oven, 375°F, for about 8 minutes, or until golden brown.

5 Remove from the oven and leave for 5 minutes to settle, then slip them out of the pan with a knife and allow to cool on a wire rack.

6 The muffins can be reheated before serving: put them on an ovenproof plate and pop them into a preheated moderate oven, 350°F, for about 5 minutes, to heat through and puff up.

If you use non-stick mini-muffin pans it's easy to get the muffins out—or, even easier, you could line them with mini paper bake cups ("bonbon" cases) which look attractive, too.

pecorino bites

egg truffle cheese

makes 12
preparation 20 minutes
cooking 20 minutes

1 lb potatoes, peeled and cut into
   even-size pieces
2 tablespoons truffle oil
1 oz Pecorino cheese, grated
1–2 teaspoons porcini mushrooms
   in a vegetarian white truffle paste
   (see page 184)
1 large egg, beaten
4–6 tablespoons dried
   bread crumbs
canola or peanut oil for deep-frying
salt and pepper, to taste

1 Cover the potatoes in boiling water and cook for about 15 minutes, or until tender. Drain thoroughly. Mash the potatoes with the truffle oil, Pecorino, and some salt and pepper. Set aside until cool enough to handle.

2 Divide the mixture into 12 equal portions. Flatten each piece, then put a small spoonful—about ⅛ of a teaspoon—of truffle paste onto the center of each. Take each of the rounds, draw the sides up so that the truffle paste is enclosed, and form into a ball shape. Dip the balls first in beaten egg and then in dried bread crumbs, so that they are completely coated.

3 Heat sufficient oil for deep-frying to 350–375°F, or until a cube of bread browns in 30 seconds, and fry the potato balls for 2–3 minutes, or until golden and crisp. Drain on paper towels. Serve hot, warm, or cold.

smoked tofu mini-skewers with satay dip

basil ginger chili

(V)

makes 32
preparation 20 minutes
cooking 20–30 minutes

2 x 7½ oz blocks smoked tofu,
   drained
1–2 tablespoons toasted
   sesame oil
small bunch of Thai basil or cilantro

for the satay dip
1 tablespoon unsweetened
   peanut butter, smooth or chunky
½ teaspoon grated fresh
   ginger root
1 garlic clove, crushed to a paste
½ x 13 oz can organic coconut milk
dried red pepper flakes
salt and pepper, to taste
mild paprika pepper, to garnish

1 Cut each block of tofu into 4 fingers, then cut each of these into 4, to make 16 cubes. Toss the cubes in the sesame oil, put onto a broiler pan and cook under a medium-hot broiler until brown and crisp all over, turning them to cook each side of the cubes. This process will take 20–30 minutes. Don't rush it—it's important to get the tofu nice and crisp.

2 Meanwhile, make the satay dip. Put the peanut butter, ginger, and garlic into a bowl and mix, then gradually stir in the coconut milk to make a smooth, thick sauce. Add a pinch or two of pepper flakes, to give it a bit of a kick, and some salt and pepper. Put into a small serving bowl and set aside.

3 Put a small Thai basil or cilantro leaf and a cube of tofu onto each of 32 toothpicks. Put the bowl of dip on a serving plate and sprinkle with a little paprika. Arrange the tofu mini-skewers around the bowl of dip and serve. The tofu can be served hot or cold.

baby yorkshire puddings
with nut roast and horseradish

herbs almonds soy

makes 24
preparation 20 minutes,
plus standing
cooking 35 minutes

½ cup all-purpose white flour
1 egg
⅓ cup milk
⅓ cup water
2 tablespoons olive oil plus extra
   for greasing
salt and pepper, to taste
horseradish sauce, to serve

for the nut roast
⅓ cup almonds
1 thin slice wholewheat bread
½ cup grated cheese
¼ cup roughly chopped onion
½ teaspoon dried mixed herbs
1 tablespoon shoyu or tamari

1 Sift the flour into a bowl with a pinch of salt. Make a well in the center, break the egg into it and mix to a paste, then gradually draw in the flour. Mix the milk with the water, then stir into the bowl, but don't over beat. Transfer the batter to a pitcher, so that it will be easy to pour into the pan, and allow to rest for 30 minutes. This allows the starch to swell, giving a lighter result.

2 Meanwhile, prepare the nut roast: put all the ingredients into a food processor and whiz until you have a smooth mixture that holds together. Form it into 24 cocktail sausages, coat all over with olive oil and place on a baking sheet.

3 Use 2 x 12-hole nonstick mini-muffin pans, each hole measuring ¾ inch across and about ¾ inch deep. Put ½ teaspoon olive oil into each hole and put the pans into a preheated oven, 425°F. The oil needs to heat for 10 minutes before you put the batter in.

4 Put the nut roast sausages in the oven at this point (they will take longer to cook than the Yorkshire puddings) and roast for about 15 minutes, or until they are brown and crisp.

5 When the oil in the muffin pans is smoking hot, quickly pour the batter into each hole, filling them about two-thirds full. Bake for 10 minutes, until puffed up and golden. Pop them out of the pan and cool on a wire rack.

6 When you want to serve the Yorkshire puddings, put them on a heatproof serving dish and place a small piece of nut roast on top of each. Put them in the oven, 425°F, for 4–5 minutes, until hot and puffy. Serve immediately with horseradish sauce.

These are fabulous, and not nearly as much work as you might think because they can be prepared in advance and then just reheated before serving—they'll puff up beautifully.

little fava bean and mint risottos

rice mint wine

serves 24
preparation 30 minutes
cooking 30 minutes

1¼ cups frozen fava beans
4 cups vegetable stock
1 tablespoon olive oil
bunch of scallions, finely chopped
2 garlic cloves, finely chopped
2 cups risotto rice
3–4 large sprigs of mint
6 tablespoons dry white wine
¼ cup butter
1⅓ cups freshly grated
  Parmesan-style cheese
salt and pepper, to taste
chopped mint, to garnish

1 Cook the fava beans in a little boiling water for 4–5 minutes, then drain and cool them. Pop the bright green beans out of their grey skins and put to one side. Discard the skins.

2 To make the risotto, put the stock into a saucepan and bring to a boil, then reduce the heat and keep the stock hot over a very gentle heat.

3 Heat the olive oil in a large saucepan, add the scallions and stir, then cover and allow to cook gently for 3–4 minutes, until tender but not browned. Stir in the garlic and cook for an additional minute or so.

4 Add the rice to the pan, along with the mint sprigs, and stir over a gentle heat for 2–3 minutes, or until the rice looks translucent, then pour in the wine and stir continuously as it bubbles away.

5 When the wine has disappeared, add a ladleful of the hot stock and stir over a low-to-medium heat until the rice has absorbed the stock. Add another ladleful and continue in this way, adding the fava beans with the final ladleful of stock, until you've used up all the stock, the rice is tender and the consistency creamy. The whole process takes 15–20 minutes.

6 Remove the sprigs of mint, add the butter and half the Parmesan and season with salt and pepper. Immediately transfer the risotto into warmed ramekins, scatter each with a little Parmesan and chopped mint and serve at once, each with a tiny spoon.

Creamy risotto, served piping hot in little ramekins with tiny spoons, makes a sensational party dish and is very easy to do.

jelly and cream spongecakes

jam cream butter

makes 20
preparation 20 minutes
cooking 15–20 minutes

½ cup butter, softened
½ cup superfine sugar
2 eggs
1 cup self-rising flour
1 teaspoon baking powder
1 tablespoon water
confectioners' sugar, to dredge

for the filling
3–4 tablespoons raspberry jelly
⅔ cup heavy cream, whipped

1 Beat together the butter, superfine sugar, eggs, flour, baking powder, and water until light and creamy.

2 Line an 8½ x 12½ inch jelly roll pan with nonstick paper and spoon the mixture in, smoothing the surface and making sure the mixture gets into the corners. Bake in a preheated oven, 325°F, for 15–20 minutes, until risen and firm to a light touch. Remove from the pan and allow to cool on a wire rack.

3 When the cake is completely cold, lay it face down on a board and carefully strip off the paper. Cut the cake into two equal halves and spread one of them with first the jelly and then the cream. Press the other half on top, gently but firmly, then use a 1½ inch plain round cutter to cut 20 circles and put them onto a plate. (They may look neatest upside down—that way if the cake on top cracks a bit as you cut it, it won't show.)

4 When the cakes are all done, dredge them with confectioners' sugar and keep them in a cool place until required.

These are like darling little Victoria spongecakes! The discarded "cuttings" of cake, jelly and cream make a great base for a quick trifle, with some fruit, custard, and jello.

pecan and tarragon-stuffed apricots

fruit nuts juice

V

makes about 26
preparation 15 minutes,
   plus soaking

1½ cups ready-to-eat dried apricots
1¼ cups apple juice
1 cup vegan herb and garlic
   cream cheese
½ cup pecan nuts
small bunch of tarragon

1 Put the apricots into a bowl, cover with the apple juice and allow to soak for 8 hours, or overnight.

2 Drain the apricots and blot with paper towels. Stuff each apricot with 1 teaspoon of cream cheese, a pecan nut, and a small sprig of tarragon. Arrange them, stuffing-side up, on a serving platter.

This is a delicious treat for your vegan party guests, though everyone will enjoy it. You can get vegan cream cheese at good healthfood stores.

berry skewers with white chocolate dip

fruit cream sauce

makes 20
preparation 15 minutes
cooking 5 minutes

1½ cups mixed berries, such as
   strawberries (halved), large
   blueberries, raspberries,
   blackberries, or baby kiwis
   (halved)

for the white chocolate dip
4 oz white chocolate, broken
   into pieces
½ cup heavy cream

1 To make the dip, melt the chocolate in a bowl set over a pan of steaming water. Remove from the heat and stir in the cream. Put into a small serving bowl and set aside to cool.

2 Put one or two berries on each small toothpick or cocktail stick—enough for a mouthful. Arrange the skewers around the bowl of white chocolate dip and serve.

With soft fruit, chocolate, and cream—you really can't lose, can you?

notes on ingredients

Almond butter Available with no added ingredients such as emulsifiers, from good healthfood stores. There is a brown version and a white one. The oil may separate in the jar—just give it a good stir before use.

Arame seaweed A delicately flavored seaweed, available dried from good healthfood stores. Simply wash and soak briefly before use.

Bergamot oil An essential oil, a small quantity of which can be used as a flavoring; available from healthfood stores.

Buckwheat Strictly speaking, a seed, though usually classified as a grain. Available from organic food stores, raw or toasted. I prefer to buy raw and, if required, toast it briefly in a dry pan before use.

Coconut milk Organic coconut milk is much nicer than the non-organic type (which has unnecessary additives) and there's no point in buying the low-fat version as it's just coconut milk with water added— you might as well buy the whole type and add your own water.

Curry leaves Can be found in some large super- markets and Indian food markets. They freeze well, so it's worth buying up a good supply of fresh ones when you see them—just pop them into the freezer and use when required.

Garam masala A mixture of ground spices added toward the end of cooking to enhance the flavor. Every keen Indian cook has their own recipe, made from spices which they roast, mix, and grind themselves, but a store-bought mixture is fine.

Kaffir lime leaves Can be bought dried, in a jar, from supermarkets; use them up quickly before they lose their magical fragrance.

Ketjap manis A type of soy sauce from Indonesia, which is sweeter and less salty than most other types. It can be found in some supermarkets. Alternatively, you can sweeten ordinary soy sauce with some honey. Store indefinitely in a cool, dry place.

Masa harina A type of cornmeal used to make tortillas. You can buy it at stockists of Mexican food and some large supermarkets.

Mirin A sweet fortified yellow Japanese wine used only for cooking. Found in Asian food stores and some large supermarkets.

Miso Fermented soy paste. Generally speaking, the lighter the miso the milder the flavor and greater the sweetness. Available from healthfood stores and Asian food stores. To get the full health benefits, buy unpasteurized miso and do not boil or overheat it in order to retain its health-giving enzymes.

Nutritional yeast Dried "inactive" yeast in the form of flakes, available in a tub from gourmet healthfood stores. It has a pleasant cheesy, nutty taste—and is rich in many nutrients.

Palm sugar A brown unrefined sugar used throughout Asia. It is available from large supermarkets and is often sold as a solid block. Dark brown sugar can be substituted.

Pastry From a health and flavor point of view, I prefer pure butter pastry. This is are unsuitable for vegans, who should use pastry made from pure vegetable fat.

Porcini mushrooms in white truffle oil Both truffle oil and porcini and white truffle paste can be found in some supermarkets or Italian food stores.

Ras el hanout A Moroccan spice mixture that you can buy at some supermarkets.

Sesame oil Dark sesame oil can be found in any supermarkets and it gives a unique and delectable flavor to Asian dishes. You need only a small amount.

Superfine sugar I like to use Fair Trade golden superfine sugar (and other ingredients) when available. Golden superfine sugar is not much different in flavor and nutritional content to the white stuff, but I find it more aesthetically pleasing!

Tahini Like peanut butter, but made from sesame seeds, without additives. I prefer the pale version which is easy to find in supermarkets and healthfood stores. It has a delectable creamy, slightly bitter flavor.

Tamari, shoyu, and soy sauce Shoyu is the Japanese word for soy sauce. It is an all-purpose flavoring enhancer; tamari is wheat-free with a stronger flavor. It's important to make sure you buy brands that are traditionally brewed, natural and organic. Available from some supermarkets and from healthfood stores.

Tamarind A long brown pod with seeds and a tangy pulp used throughout Asia as a souring ingredient. Tamarind paste can be bought in jars in Indian markets and some supermarkets. Lemon juice may be substituted.

Tofu Tofu is found in the chilled food section of many supermarkets. The type most widely available is "firm." I've mostly used this in the recipes because it's a reliable all-purpose type of tofu, suitable for slicing and frying or, with liquid added, for making into a dip or dressing. You can buy other fine, delicate types of tofu in Asian food and organic stores and these are delicious and worth experimenting with if you like tofu.

Toover dahl Also called toor dhal, this is a small golden legume. It has an earthy, almost smoky flavor and makes a beautiful dhal. Sometimes it's coated in oil to preserve it—wash this off by rinsing it in hot water before cooking. Golden split peas would be the best substitute.

Umeboshi plums/umeboshi paste These have a delicious salty sharpness that enhances many foods. Refrigerated, they will last for ages in their jar. Buy from gourmet healthfood stores.

Unsweetened soy cream Cartons of soy cream equivalent to light cream can be found in healthfood stores and supermarkets in the UK. It does contain a little sugar, but not enough to make it "sweet"— check the label. In the USA it is not so easy to find: substitute unsweetened soy milk, which has a creamy consistency when cooked. A ready-whipped soy cream in an aerosol, and another that you can whip yourself, have recently become available—I find them overly sweet.

Vegetarian Worcester sauce Can be bought from healthfood stores. (The problem with ordinary Worcestershire sauce is that it contains anchovy extract.)

Vinegars While you can get away with just one type of vinegar—I'd choose organic cider vinegar—it's useful to have two or three different ones. Rice vinegar is light and suitable for Chinese and Japanese dishes, while Balsamic has a wonderfully rich, sweet flavor: the more you spend on it, the better it will be.

Wakame seaweed A leafy seaweed, a bit like spinach to look at and with a mild, yummy flavor of the sea. Available dried from gourmet healthfood stores.

Wasabi A strong green Japanese horseradish condiment with a hot mustard taste. It is available as a powder or a paste in some supermarkets and Asian food stores. English mustard can be substituted.

Wild mushrooms Supermarket wild mushroom mixtures can be good value, though for a real treat and a no-expense-spared meal nothing can replace a few precious chanterelles, morels, or some fresh porcini. Although they're very expensive, because they weigh very little you get a lot for your money. Dried mushrooms are good value—I especially like dried morels that you can buy at some supermarkets.

Frying

The healthiest way to deep-fry is to use canola or peanut oils, which are stable at high temperatures (and therefore healthier), and discard them after use. I use a wok, which has a large surface area so you use less oil or, if I'm doing just a little frying, a small saucepan. For pan-frying and roasting I generally use olive oil, which is my standard all-purpose oil, but you should refer to the individual recipe.

To broil and skin a sweet pepper

To broil and skin a sweet pepper, cut the pepper in half and remove the core, stem, and seeds. Place the halves rounded-side up on a broiler pan and broil on high for about 10 minutes, or until the skin is blistered and black in places and the flesh tender. Remove from the heat and allow to cool, then peel off the skin.

Toasting hazelnuts

If you're starting with the skinned type (which are the most widely available), either toast them under a hot broiler for a few minutes, stirring them after 1–2 minutes so they toast evenly, or put them on a baking sheet and roast in a moderate oven—350°F. They'll take only 8–10 minutes, so watch them carefully and remove them from the hot baking sheet immediately they're done so they don't go on browning. To toast unskinned hazelnuts, that is, those still in their brown skins, proceed as described, but they'll take about 20 minutes in the oven. Let them cool, then rub off the brown skins with your fingers or a soft cloth.

Vegan recipes

Many of the recipes in this book are naturally vegan and are labeled as such. A lot more can easily be made vegan by making simple substitutions such as using olive oil or vegan margarine instead of butter, soy instead of dairy cream, maple syrup instead of honey, and vegan puff pastry (read the label) instead of all-butter puff pastry. Here are some suggested vegan alternatives:

Non-vegan	Vegan
butter	vegan margarine
milk	soy milk
cream	soy cream
yogurt	soy yogurt
cream cheese	vegan cream cheese
goat cheese	vegan cream cheese
feta cheese	vegan feta cheese
cheddar (or other firm) cheese	vegan cheddar (or other firm) cheese
Parmesan-style cheese (grated)	vegan Parmesan cheese
paneer	firm tofu or firm vegan cheese
mayonnaise	vegan mayonnaise
hollandaise sauce	vegan mayonnaise
honey	maple syrup

menu plans

Barbecue
Green olives with mixed peppercorns and
coriander (V) *(see page 152)*
Spice-crusted tofu with maple glaze (V) *(see page 136)*
Zucchini and corn cakes with chili sauce (V)
(see page 128)
Lemon-glazed and seared halloumi with herb salad
(see page 86)
Buckwheat and mango tabbouleh (V) *(see page 151)*
Sangria fruit salad with almond shortbreads
(see page 116)

Family meal
Roast potatoes in sea salt and balsamic vinegar (V)
(see page 48)
Chickpea flatcake topped with lemon- and honey-
roasted vegetables *(see page 65)*
Strawberries in rose jello (V) *(see page 115)*

Garden celebration menu
Bloody Mary jellos *(see page 32)*
Salad of warm artichokes and chanterelles
(see page 15)
Individual pea, spinach, and mint pithiviers
(see page 78)
Parsnips in sage butter *(see page 46)*
Pink Champagne granita marbled with raspberries (V)
(see page 118)

Romantic supper
Sesame-roasted asparagus with wasabi vinaigrette (V)
(see page 38)
Brie and cranberry soufflés *(see page 76)*
Melting chocolate puddings *(see page 96)*

Impromptu supper
Crisp tofu with tomato and lemon grass sambal (V)
(see page 37)
Rice noodles with chili-ginger vegetables (V)
(see page 56)
Nectarines roasted with lavender *(see page 114)*

Informal meal
Polenta fry stack with dipping sauces (V)
(see page 40)
Bubble-and-squeak cakes with beet relish
(see page 68)
White chocolate gelato with citrus drizzle
(see page 121)

New Year party buffet
Smoked tofu mini-skewers with satay dip (V)
(see page 175)
Baby Yorkshire puddings with nut roast and
horseradish *(see page 176)*
Little fava bean and mint risottos *(see page 178)*
Jelly and cream spongecakes *(see page 180)*
Berry skewers with white chocolate dip
(see page 182)

Supper for friends
Rosemary sorbet (V) *(see page 26)*
Refritos gateau *(see page 71)*
Fruit fajita pudding *(see page 158)*

Thanksgiving/Festive dinner
Canapés: bruschette with three toppings
(see page 162)
Tomato and Parmesan tarts with basil cream
(see page 36)
Carrot, parsnip, and chestnut terrine with red wine
gravy *(see page 92)*
Cabbage with sesame and ginger (V) *(see page 46)*
Fig tarte tatin with ginger cream *(see page 104)*

Vegan feast
Chilled melon soup with mint granita (V) *(see page 24)*
Portobello steaks en croûte *(see page 84)*
Braised whole baby carrots and fennel (V)
(see page 44)
Coconut and kaffir lime panna cotta (V) *(see page 112)*

index

acknowledgments

Writing a book like this would not be possible without the help and expertise of many people and I would like to thank them all. Firstly, my wonderful editor, Sarah Ford, for having the idea and contributing many wonderful, mouthwatering ideas, and Alison Goff for her enthusiasm and support for the project. I would also like to say a special, big thank you to my daughter Claire who, as luck would have it, was at home while I was writing this book and her taste buds, editing skills and creativity were invaluable. I would like to thank Jason Lowe for the fantastic photographs of the food, and Sunil Vijayakar for cooking the food so beautifully and Mary for helping him so ably; also the editorial team: Jessica Cowie, Barbara Dixon (it was so nice to work with you again, Barbara) and Jo Lethaby. A huge thank you, too, to the art department, especially Tracy Killick and Joanna MacGregor, for producing such a beautiful design and making this book look so attractive. Thanks, too, to my agent, Barbara Levy, and to my dear husband for his unwavering support and help.

Executive Editor **Sarah Ford**
Senior Editor **Jessica Cowie**
Executive Art Editor **Joanna MacGregor**
Design **Grade Design Consultants,
London**
Production Manager **Ian Paton**

Photography **Jason Lowe** © Octopus
Publishing Group Limited
Food Stylist **Sunil Vijayakar**
Prop Stylist **Rachel Jukes**

The Publishers would like to thank Ceramica Blue, 10 Blenheim Crescent, London W11 1NN for the kind loan of some of the props for photography.